THE STORY OF KINMEL PARK
MILITARY TRAINING CAMP
1914–1918

To Les,

A fine man with close

connections to Bodelwyddan

and Kinmel Park Camp – Bob.

Robert H. Griffiths.

The Story of Kinmel Park Military Training Camp 1914–1918

Robert H. Griffiths

First published in 2014

© Robert H. Griffiths

© Llygad Gwalch 2014

ISBN: 978-1-84524-218-3

Cover design: Eleri Owen

Published by Gwasg Carreg Gwalch,
12 Iard yr Orsaf, Llanrwst, Wales LL26 0EH
tel: 01492 642031
fax: 01492 641502
email: books@carreg-gwalch.com
website: www.carreg-gwalch.com

To my very special wife, Ruth

Without her support, assistance and forbearance
this book would never have seen the light of day

This book is dedicated to four people all directly involved in the Great War. The four departed this earth many years ago, one at the tender age of eighteen, but all are most certainly not forgotten by their descendants:

My grandfather, Leonard Price (1897–1975), of Southsea, near Wrexham, a private in the Royal Welch Fusiliers, Regimental Number 8607 and later 201152, who as a young man saw active service in France and Flanders, including at the Third Battle of Ypres.

My grandmother, Margaret Alice Price (nee Ellis) (1900–1972), of Southsea, near Wrexham, who as a very young woman served in France with the Women's Army Auxiliary Corps (WAAC), renamed in April 1918 the Queen Mary's Army Auxiliary Corps (QMAAC), and rode a white horse up and down the lines delivering messages.

My wife's paternal Taid, Thomas Jones (1892–1970), of Groes, near Denbigh, who served in firstly 9th and then 4th Battalion, the South Wales Borderers, Regimental Number 27552. He received his initial military training at Kinmel Park Camp and later saw active service in Mesopotamia and Egypt, surviving on one occasion being bayoneted in the face by an enemy soldier.

My wife's great-uncle, Robert Owen (1898–1916), of Mallwyd, Dinas Mawddwy, a private in 20th Reserve Battalion, the Royal Welch Fusiliers, Regimental Number 37022. He did not live to complete his initial military training at Kinmel Park Camp, but died at the age of eighteen. He was the inspiration for me to embark upon the writing of this book some ten years ago.

(Discovered on a postcard probably first issued between late 1916 and early 1917)

'Down In Our Kinmel Park Camp'
To the tune of 'Back Home In Tennessee'

I'm so lonely, oh so lonely,
In our Blinking Camp,
I'm like a bloomin'tramp,
Not worth a penny stamp,
Father, Mother, Sister, Brother,
All are waiting me,
I'm getting thinner, miss my dinner
And my Sunday's tea.

CHORUS:

Down in our Blinking Camp,
We're always on the ramp,
That's where we cop the cramp,
Through sleeping in the damp,
All we can hear there each day,
Is Left ... Right ... march away,
Sergeants calling, Lance-jacks bawling
'Get out On Parade'.
We go to bed at night,
It is a glorious sight,
The earwigs on the floor,
Double-up and then Form Fours,
Then when daylight is dawning,
You can hear our Sergeant yawnin'
Show-a-leg there, Show-a-leg there,
Down in our Kinmel Camp.

Contents

Foreword

Bob Morris

The First World War was one of the greatest tragedies in history. It is something of a cliché today to say that 'the world changed' at a particular moment in time. It certainly did so in 1914. The aggressive posturing of Europe's great powers, their imperial expansion overseas and a frenetic pace of economic and military competition had, by 1914, created an explosive political hothouse.

All the same, few people in Britain in June 1914 thought that the assassination of Archduke Franz Ferdinand and Archduchess Sophie in Sarajevo would set all this dry tinder alight. Yet that is exactly what happened. Within a mere six weeks, most of Europe was at war; and the ensuing Armageddon would last for four bitter years. It would bring four historic empires tumbling down and transform the map of Europe and the Middle East forever.

Most importantly and most tragically, the years of carnage would cost some 20 million lives, 750,000 of them from Britain. Many of them were young men who had flocked to join their countries' forces in a passion of patriotism and a sense of shared adventure.

They would, indeed, share much, but the lasting memories of those who survived the war would not be the adventure but the loss of those friends who, in the words of Laurence Binyon's famous poem, 'shall grow not old'. Even in extreme old age, the last veterans of the Great War would remember the fallen comrades of their youth above all else.

Some historians have written of the outbreak of the Great War as being born of logistics, of the demands of railway timetables and transport arrangements for the millions of troops which the great European powers had raised. It was one of those logistical considerations, as Germany faced the imminence of a full Russian army in the field on the Eastern Front within some two months, which prompted the German High Command to send an army through Belgium in August 1914. This bid to defeat France quickly across undefended territory meant violating Belgium's 'perpetual neutrality', a status which had been guaranteed by international treaty since 1839.

The invasion of 'gallant little Belgium' by Germany and the trampling of the so-called 'Scrap of Paper' underfoot was crucial in bringing Britain into the war. David Lloyd George, the Chancellor of the Exchequer, spoke for many when he referred to the war as a struggle to defend the 'five-foot-two nations', such as the embattled Belgium and Serbia.

This remarkable book by Robert Griffiths deals with some of the consequences of those dramatic events in the summer of 1914, and particularly the part that north Wales played in them. Kinmel Camp had a vital place in the lives of thousands of men who served in the Great War and in the lives of their families. It became the training camp for soldiers, from all over Wales, who enlisted in infantry regiments such as the Royal Welsh Fusiliers, the South Wales Borderers and the Welsh Regiment, although the home barracks of their regular battalions were in Wrexham and Caernarfon (RWF), Brecon (SWB) and Cardiff (WR).

Kinmel was also seen, initially, as the home depôt for the new 'Welsh Army Corps', originally proposed by Lloyd George and formally established in October 1914. This scheme extended the popular, though ultimately tragic, concept of the 'Pals' Battalions' into a national infantry corps for Wales. The recruits came to Kinmel from all over Wales, and a high proportion from the north Wales counties, which were the traditional recruiting ground of the Royal Welch Fusiliers. The camp soon extended its scope, however, to provide training and supply recruits for many front-line divisions in the field.

Robert Griffiths has spent many years researching the story of Kinmel Camp, the people who passed through it – including many who died in the camp – and the lives of families and communities which were deeply affected by it and by what happened there. The author and I both remember hearing family stories about the young recruits who served at Kinmel, some of whom died in training, and of mysterious references to a 'German doctor' wreaking havoc at the camp. The mutiny among Canadian troops awaiting repatriation there in 1919, and its tragic consequences, is a more widely-known episode, and one of many sad epitaphs to the bloody saga of the Great War. Robert Griffiths has investigated and illuminated these controversial events and the result is a fascinating study.

This book brings the broader story of Kinmel Camp into sharp relief. With a passion for truth, a deep commitment to thorough research and a strong sympathy for the ordinary people portrayed here – people carried on powerful currents that they had no hope of controlling – Robert Griffiths has brought together a host of human stories about Kinmel Camp and its people. Nor has he confined himself to the camp alone, but he has shown us the impact of war on neighbouring communities such as Bodelwyddan, Rhyl and Abergele, which lived cheek-by-jowl with this sprawling encampment that dwarfed all three of them.

The pathos and tragedy of war are certainly here, but so are some of the lighter moments that the recruits enjoyed when the day's training was done. So also is the astonishing courage and resilience of many of those who passed through Kinmel on the way to battle – battles from which many would not return. As Wilfred Owen wrote of another camp and another departure:

Down the close, darkening lanes they sang their way
To the siding shed,
And lined the train with faces grimly gay ...
Shall they return to beatings of great bells
In wild train-loads?
A few, a few, too few for drums and yells.

'The Send-Off', Wilfred Owen, 1893–1918

And they went, not only to France and Belgium – to places that became by-words for tragic heroism, like Mametz and Passchendaele, Festubert and Neuve Chapelle – but also to Gallipoli, Kut al-Amara and Palestine. Many of them went, in the words of the poet Robert Williams Parry, whose heartfelt verse commemorated so many of his fallen friends:

I Ffrainc, i'r Aifft, i Ganaan, i hir hedd.

[To France, to Egypt, to Canaan, to eternal peace.]

'Y Ddrafft' (The Draft), Robert Williams Parry
(From *Yr Haf a Cherddi Eraill*, Gwasg Gee
(1970, xxxix, p. 99)

The colourful tapestry that Robert Griffiths has woven, from the wealth of human testimony that he has explored, will enrich our understanding of the Great War and the people who were drawn into it. This contribution is especially important today, as we start to commemorate the centenary of the conflict. Those of us who are 'of a certain age' grew up knowing people who had served in the Great War. They might have been soldiers, sailors, airmen, munitionettes, nurses or land-girls. They are all gone now, and our children and grandchildren will not have the privilege of knowing any of them personally.

Books like this one and dedicated researchers like Robert Griffiths have a vital role to play in preserving the memory of what those vanished heroes and heroines saw, what they endured and what they accomplished. Part of the fascination of the story is that there was, at Kinmel, a heady mix of saints and sinners among the thousands who went through its gates. They were people like us, but in a time very different from ours.

The now-defunct *News of the World* used to display, as its advertising strap-line, the claim: 'All human life is there'. When you have read this book and the remarkable and poignant stories of Kinmel Camp and its people, you too, will feel that you have watched a vivid and tumultuous pageant of people and experiences go by:

These hearts were woven of human joys and cares,
Washed marvelllously with sorrow, swift to mirth.
The years had given them kindness. Dawn was theirs,
And sunset, and the colours of the earth.

'1914 IV. The Dead', Rupert Brooke, 1887–1915

Bob Morris
Historian and Author

Introduction

This is an account of life, and death, in and around the Kinmel Park Military Training Camp, north Wales, 1914 to 1918, and what befell a few of the many thousands of soldiers and civilians who were stationed at, based at, or in detention at the camp.

The site of the camp went from being lush parkland to becoming the largest military training Camp in Wales during the Great War, even having its own railway, the Kinmel Camp Railway (KCR), which ran right into the centre of the camp itself, between the hutments.

Kinmel Park Camp's principal function was the training of soldiers for active military service, though in reality it also became a place of convalescence for large numbers of wounded soldiers, a place of temporary detention for many Conscientious Objectors, and a great deal more.

I have endeavoured to encompass in this book as many varied aspects of everyday life in and around the camp as possible. There are so many different stories to be told. I have tried to include a wide spectrum of the layers of society that existed at that time.

Long before the erroneously named 'Spanish Flu' pandemic swept the entire world, taking a heavy toll at Kinmel Park Camp (particularly upon the Canadian soldiers housed there awaiting repatriation to their own country), the camp had acquired a reputation as a place where too many soldiers were dying from illnesses contracted there. The camp acquired some widely known and unflattering nicknames such as 'Kill 'em Park', as stated by Winston Graham (who wrote the very successful *Poldark* novels). Soldiers, many of them young, living in unsanitary and cramped conditions, succumbed to illnesses or infections. And it should not be forgotten that the camp had quite a number of deaths from accidents and suicides.

I have over the past ten years amassed a vast amount of material on the soldiers, WAACs, nurses and civilians who were at Kinmel Camp during the First World War. There is far too much for it all to be included in this book, but I intend that sometime in the future it will appear in some form in the public domain.

This book has truly been a labour of love for me, a real passion that at times has threatened to consume all of my spare time and most of my thoughts during the waking hours. My aim has been to ensure that the people contained in this book are remembered – mostly reverently – and not just to leave them as mere names on a long forgotten gravestone or upon a war memorial that is venerated but once a year. For those, however, who managed to survive the Great War, there are no tangible reminders of their service and sacrifice, many going to their graves without even close family members knowing what they had been through – that was the way of things then.

When looking today at those few precious old pieces of Great War film footage, in grimy monochrome and with the staccato movements of their human subjects, it is easy to think of that period as being bland and lacking in colour. The reality is that the murderous and barbaric mechanised slaughter that was the Great War was fought in the bright colours that we have today ... though on reflection, perhaps the sheer hell of it, especially the murderous trench warfare, deserves to be seen by us and future generations in sepia and ghostlike – a nightmare that mankind put itself through.

The Great War was supposed to have been 'the war to end all wars', yet mankind did not learn from it, it doing nothing more than to sow the seeds for an even more destructive worldwide conflict just twenty-one years later.

My heartfelt thanks to my editor, Dr Jen Llywelyn of Gwasg Carreg Gwalch, for whom it has been a case of what to omit from the vast amount of text I originally submitted to her. I very much appreciate her diligent work on this book.

Robert H. Griffiths
Denbigh, Spring 2014

1

The Building of Kinmel Park Camp

By November of 1914 arrangements had been finalised for the building of a large military training camp near Rhyl in north Wales. It was initially intended only for the training of the Welsh Army Corps, to be built on fields in two sections, one being at Kinmel Park and the other at Bodelwyddan Park. A 2-foot gauge railway was to be built by Messrs Alban Richards from Foryd station, near Kinmel Bay, to the proposed new camp for the use of the main building contractors, Robert McAlpine and Sons. This railway would carry many of the materials needed for the construction of the new camp, which was to consist of numerous wooden huts.

At this early stage of the war on the north Wales coast, soldiers were billeted in and around the various seaside towns, including Colwyn Bay, Llandudno and Rhyl, many in temporary canvas accommodation, including a large canvas camp at nearby St Asaph. It was planned that once built, this new two-section military camp would primarily provide soldiers with a certain amount of military training before they were sent to other military camps for field operations, and then overseas in drafts to the battle zones. The general belief in these early days of the war was that it would 'all be over by Christmas' (1914), and it was not envisaged that this new military camp would need to be in existence for all that long, or that it would develop and vastly grow in size, as it most certainly did. Only some three months earlier, on 4 August 1914, Britain declared war on Germany following the totally unprovoked German invasion of neutral Belgium. On the following day, Kitchener was appointed as the Secretary of War; less than two weeks later the British Expeditionary Force (BEF) was sent to France.

The first military contact between British and German troops was at the battle of Mons, which began on 23 August 1914. The BEF at this time consisted of regular troops and some Territorials, with conscription being well over a year away. The British military leadership firmly believed that the war would be quickly won by them, but this notion was to be soon dispelled. The early optimism faded after firstly the battle of Mons and then the battle of the Marne had taken place. The result of these two battles was a bloody stalemate, and both sides literally dug in for trench warfare. The war escalated, with other countries joining the Allies (including Britain), or the Central Powers (including Germany). On 5 November 1914, Britain and France declared war on Turkey; more and more countries were being dragged into it, on one side or the other. The German attack upon Belgium had clearly shown that a country declaring itself as neutral in this war was no guarantee of it being kept out of the conflict.

The Building of Kinmel Park Military Training Camp
By the last week of November 1914 all the available labourers in the town of Rhyl and its outlying districts had been engaged for the work of erecting the numerous wooden huts, to serve as barracks at both the Kinmel and Bodelwyddan military camp sites (the camp would become known both officially and unofficially as Kinmel Park Camp). A Mr W. H. Jones of Penybont had been engaged to carry out the drainage work that was required. At this stage, the sites for the two camps were nothing more than bare fields. The local press reported that it was anticipated that the soldiers then billeted at Rhyl, Llandudno and other north Wales coastal resorts would be transferred to the

wooden hut barracks at the Kinmel and Bodelwyddan sites, just as soon as they were completed.

This information did not, of course, please everybody, as the lodging-house keepers of the north Wales coastal resorts were to lose valuable income once the new camp opened. This was wintertime and the best months for the lodging houses were the summer months, with holidaymakers thronging to the seaside towns. It was at this time that Lieutenant-Colonel (later Brigadier General) Owen Thomas, who was in command of the Caernarvonshire and Anglesey units of the Welsh Brigade, informed (reported in the press) the Llandudno Urban District Council, that the billeting allowance approved by Lord Kitchener and the War Office was 3s 4½d per day and not 2s per man as had apparently been previously reported in the press. Lieutenant-Colonel Owen Thomas pointed out that the higher figure was already being paid to lodging-house keepers in the Rhyl area, to enable them to cater satisfactorily for the soldiers billeted with them, but also to have some money left for their time and trouble. Rhyl had become a military centre of some importance prior to November of 1914, as it was the quarters for the South Wales Brigade of the Welsh Army Corps, who would often carry out drills and parades on the Rhyl Promenade.

A corps of Royal Engineers also arrived at the Kinmel and Bodelwyddan sites to assist in the construction of the camp. These men were billeted in the locality at Abergele, Rhuddlan and St George. Local businessmen began to realise how financially lucrative it could be to have a military camp on their doorsteps, filled with thousands of soldiers with money in their pockets. Already the towns and villages in the area were feeling the changes in lifestyle and noise, as this large military camp was being built and soon to be opened in their locality. Life for the local people would not be the same for over five years.

A rather hopeful target of only six weeks had been set for the completion of the erecting of the wooden huts to act as barracks and for the first soldiers to actually live in them. This really was difficult when one considers the scale of the task, and that the work was being carried out in the winter.

The subject of providing a water supply for the camp, for the envisaged thousands of troops to be stationed at the Kinmel Park site, was discussed at a meeting in November 1914 of the Rural District Council. Dr Lloyd, the council's medical officer, pointed out that it would be necessary to take some precautions to ensure that satisfactory sanitation arrangements were put in place, in addition to an efficient supply of clean water to the new camp. Opinion was also that if the water supply was to be tapped at Bodelwyddan, then it would adversely affect the water supply at nearby Llanddulas. It was suggested that the water supply be drawn from nearby Glascoed. The Local Government Board wrote inviting the co-operation of the council's sanitary inspector with a view to the effective control of infections, diseases and the disposal of refuse from the new camp. It was resolved to give Dr Lloyd full powers to deal with these matters and to liaise with the military authorities.

By the beginning of December 1914, all the timber for the wooden huts had arrived at the nearby Abergele/Pensarn railway station. Many manual workers were employed for the heavy loading and unloading work that was required.

It had already become evident that the initial idea – that the new camp with its hut barracks would be provided purely for the Welsh Army Corps – had now changed. Now, according to General Dunn, something altogether different was being envisaged: the new camp would actually be for a brigade of some 18,000 to 20,000 soldiers who had hitherto been in training at 'canvas camps' in other parts of the country. Perhaps this was a result of the realisation that this war would not be quickly won, and most certainly not 'over by Christmas'.

Tradesmen Required

This advertisement appeared first in the *Denbighshire Free Press* on Saturday 5 December 1914, and also in several subsequent editions:

SITUATIONS VACANT
Wanted at once: Carpenters, Sheeters and Labourers
Apply Works Manager, Rhyl Camp, Abergele

Local news relating to Kinmel Park Camp

In early December 1914, a meeting was held of the Abergele Temperance Society in order to discuss the entertainment of the troops at the forthcoming military training camp at the Kinmel Park and Bodelwyddan Park sites. The Society decided to request that the chief constable of the county of Denbigh restrict the hours in which intoxicating liquor could be sold or consumed in the licensed premises in their area. They feared that the late opening of such licensed premises would be a great temptation to the men to stay in the town of Abergele until unreasonably late hours.

The above sentiments were almost certainly not, in the coming months, supported in any shape or form by the majority of the soldiers based at the camp, or by local licensees.

By late December 1914, a large number of workmen were working night and day at the site. There was still a great demand for joiners who were said to be paid 10½d. per hour. But even at this decent rate of pay, men were difficult to get.

Work at the camp continued apace, despite awful winter

weather. At the end of the first week of January 1915, twelve rows of wooden huts divided by parades had been erected. Each of the huts was 30 feet by 20 feet. Twenty huts in each row, with their gable ends pointing to the parades. Already more land was required for the camp and this was speedily obtained by the military authorities.

In this same first week of January 1915, unrest among the many workers at the camp was fermenting. A mass meeting of the carpenters was held at the local National School, at which they complained of having to work in unfavourable conditions and particularly at being required to work on Sundays, which they believed should be a day of rest, whether or not they were religious men. The tremendous consignments of timber required for the new camp had to be transported from the railway station at Pensarn to the Kinmel Park site. Traction engines had to be chartered from outside the district for this heavy hauling work. The work of loading and unloading also took place on Sundays. The military authorities promptly promised to investigate these complaints.

A number of local people also complained, either in writing to the Home Office or by venting their anger in the local press, concerning the negative effects the camp was having on their lives, particularly on Sundays. Complaints were made by locals seeing roughly-clad workmen travelling to and from the new camp, many in large charabancs, and making a lot of noise with their hammers and saws. For some locally the sight and sound of noisy and heavy traction engines puffing along the roads on the Sabbath was not only unusual but also unacceptable. Many questioned the necessity of Sunday working and considered that men were being coerced into working on Sundays. It was wartime, but for many locals, even patriotic ones, 'the war' was being fought in far-off places, so why should it impinge on their hitherto peaceful lifestyles?

Enough complaints were made to force the military authorities representative to write a piece which was published in the local newspapers. He stated that 'no belt had been used to make workers work on the Sabbath, it was only the draw of double pay for Sunday working'.

In mid-February 1915, the *Abergele and Pensarn Visitor* carried a letter to the editor, from a joiner working locally. In his letter he made a complaint:

> Locally [he meant at Abergele], shopkeepers have increased their prices for goods, due to the large numbers of workers now engaged in the locality, at the new Kinmel Park Camp, local prices having increased enough for shoppers to shop at nearby Pensarn instead.

Another letter to a local paper blamed rising prices on 'the Landlords who are piling on a big advance in their rents for the next quarter', and in another, a mother of six children stated that she no longer shopped in Abergele, but instead shopped at the next town for her goods, apparently saving her about six shillings per week. She finished her letter with these vitriolic words: 'No more daylight robbery for me, the biggest over-chargers are the biggest Christians on a Sunday.'

The Kinmel Camp Railway (the KCR)

With the military training camp being established at Kinmel Park, transport links needed to be improved quickly. Plenty of fairly flat land had been made available for the construction of the camp, but it was poorly located for transport reasons. So at a very early stage the War Department decided to construct a railway line to connect the new camp with the main Chester to Holyhead line. At this time this railway line was to be built purely to facilitate the construction work, especially the carrying of construction materials and thereby aiding the early completion of the camp. At this time there was no thought whatsoever of it having any role in the transport of passengers, whether military or civilian. Eventually a spur of the KCR ran right through the middle of the camp, running parallel to the main road that traversed the camp, the spur reaching as far as the Camp 9 headquarters and almost to Camp 10, which became the military hospital.

This railway was built across the Rhuddlan Marsh from a junction with the main Chester to Holyhead Line at Foryd station, near to Kinmel Bay. By December 1914, work had progressed well on building this railway line on the junction with the London & North Western Railway at the east end of Foryd station.

The railway line was laid at or very near ground level, crossing the Rhuddlan marsh drainage ditches by means of culverts. The line also on the level crossed the Abergele to Rhuddlan road and the St Asaph to Abergele road. The route of the line meant that no significant earthworks were required for its construction, so its building proceeded rapidly. This first line to link the Kinmel Park Camp and a main railway line was completed in February of 1915. One vital piece of construction work, however, was required, namely a small single-span bridge to be built over the river Gele.

At this time a shed was provided for three locomotives at the Foryd end of the line. It is also known that several 2' gauge locomotives were also employed around Kinmel Camp and on the KCR. These included a small-coupled well tank, works number 1129, built by Hudswell Clarke and supplied new by Robert Hudson Limited in 1915. This locomotive had 5' by 8" cylinders and 1' 8" diameter wheels.

Several of this particular type of locomotive were built by Hudswell Clarke specifically for use on the construction of military camps and aerodromes in order to fulfil War Department contracts during the period 1914 to 1918.

PERSONS WANTED
NAVVIES immediately: Sub daily.
– Apply W. Alban Richards, Army Camp, Rhyl.

Liverpool Echo, 16 August 1915

In October of 1915, with Kinmel Camp growing in size and the number of soldiers and civilian staff steadily increasing, the KCR was extended across the Bodelwyddan to Glascoed Road on the level for a further extension to the camp in Bodelwyddan Park, to the east of Kinmel Park. During 1915 and 1916, many road accidents had occurred in the area due to the high level of traffic to and from the camp, on mainly country roads as has been previously stated, that were not up to the new volumes of usage. Up to August of 1916, the KCR was used mainly for the carrying of materials for the construction of the camp. Troop arrivals and departures were continuing via the roads from Kinmel Camp to local railway stations on the main line, particularly Abergele/Pensarn and Rhyl. Many of the drafts leaving the camp for the Front did so on foot to the local railway station.

By mid-1916, with the camp construction virtually completed, the War Department unofficially now took over the running of the KCR. As a result of this in October 1916, W. Alban Richards & Company advertised for sale five locomotives that had formerly seen service on the construction of Kinmel Camp and the KCR.

With the War Department officially taking over the running of the KCR on 7 August 1916, it was thought more advantageous to have a more direct link between Kinmel Camp and the main line, so plans were drawn up for such a thing to happen. The local newspapers in September 1916 carried the story that a new light railway line was to be constructed between Kinmel Camp and Foryd station. This presumably referred to the reconstruction of the original contractor's railway line for War Department use. This 'new railway line' was completed by the end of October 1916, with goods traffic to and from Kinmel Camp being placed under the Rhyl Goods Agency from 1 November 1916. This date probably being the date of the opening of the reconstructed line. Now the large amounts of supplies required for the day-to-day running of this rapidly burgeoning camp could be brought in by train rather than by road.

It was soon realised that the interchange of railway traffic with the London & North Western Railway line at Foryd station, despite the improvements having been made to it, were unsatisfactory for the long term. So a deviation of the northern section of the railway was provided, to enable through running to and from the town of Rhyl. This new line crossed the Kinmel Bay to Bodelwyddan Road on the level, to a new connection with the Vale of Clwyd Line at Foryd Junction. This new connection was provided by the London & North Western Railway in April 1917 and was actually made with the Foryd Harbour branch. This was not straightforward, as at that time trains had to make a double reversal between the KCR and the main line. With the completion of the new Northern Section of the line, through services to Rhyl were introduced.

This led on 14 June 1917 to the KCR being officially opened for passenger traffic. The opening ceremony was performed by Sir Pitcairn Campbell, General Officer

Commanding-in-Chief of Western Command. Accounts of this opening ceremony appeared in a number of local newspapers, including the *Rhyl Journal* of Saturday 23 June 1917, when the writer waxed lyrical about this new connection between Rhyl and Kinmel Camp and asked if it could be of assistance to the local civilian population, especially business people.

The first timetable for passenger services allowed for six Monday to Saturday daily departures from Kinmel Camp to Rhyl, with seven return departures from Rhyl back to the camp. The KCR operated a curtailed train service on a Sunday, with only three trains departing for Rhyl and three returning to the camp. According to a local newspaper, the 11.25 p.m. train back to the camp was 'more often than not, especially on Friday and Saturday nights, the last train back from Rhyl is always packed to the rafters, some soldiers even riding on top of the carriages'.

Post-Armistice, the thousands of Canadian soldiers being transported in and out of Kinmel Camp prompted a local newspaper to remark that 'local people have reported seeing trains very heavily laden with vast numbers of Canadian troops arriving and departing Kinmel Camp'. These KCR trains allowed a rather leisurely thirty-five minutes for the four-mile trip between the camp and Rhyl, with three level crossings to be negotiated and the double reversal for trains travelling in opposite directions to be able to pass one another at Foryd Junction.

A mile away from the camp, on a spur line with a loop, was the Faenol Bach station. Another spur line with a run-round loop had a 236-foot long platform, and was where the War Department locomotive shed was situated. This spur line ran parallel to the St Asaph to Abergele road, passing Camp 10, and continuing into Bodelwyddan Park by the aid of a level crossing over the Bodelwyddan to Glascoed Road.

The main KCR line with a loop climbed a fairly steep gradient and reached the southern part of the camp, between Camps 14 and 15, near to Coed Pen y Garreg.

Kinmel Park Camp News

It was reported in the local press in February 1915, that soldiers, some 15,000 of them, were to start arriving at Kinmel Camp the next month.

Meanwhile, it had been decided that local farmers should be paid to remove the offal and refuse from the new camp, called 'scavenging from the camp'. Tenders were requested for this 'scavenging work'.

The YMCA at Kinmel Park Camp

The Young Men's Christian Association (YMCA) is also known around the world today simply as 'the Y'.

When war broke out in August 1914, the priority for the British YMCA was to build, establish and run YMCA huts in British military camps large and small, then the setting up of other YMCA establishments such as hostels, in the towns and cities of Britain, especially near to main railway stations or other places where there would be large gatherings of military personnel. Quickly they branched out into France, all the war zones of Europe, then into the Middle East and Africa. At most of these, YMCA huts (some of which were huge 'temporary type' buildings), military personnel, especially soldiers, were provided with hot food and drink and places for rest. Many had recreational facilities. They also operated mobile refreshments facilities, sometimes quite close to the Front.

Very soon after the completion of Kinmel Camp, the YMCA became an integral part of everyday life, especially recreation, for the many thousands of soldiers who were based there, or temporarily there for military training. The

YMCA also, later in the war, specifically benefited the women at the camp, which included members of the WAAC and nurses from the different nursing organisations.

At Kinmel Camp the YMCA had three separate hutment establishments, one much larger and with far more facilities than the other two.

At Camp 4, the YMCA had an enormous Central Pavilion that had not only a huge concert hall and cinema, but also separate rooms for different purposes:

- The main concert hall and cinema that could hold 1,000 people.
- A writing room with YMCA post office and a savings bank counter.
- A refreshment buffet and bookstall room. This had a long tea bar counter.
- A billiards room, with six full-size tables, with over-the-table lights hanging down from the room's ceiling over each table. Around the entire outside of this room were chairs for watching the games, or just relaxing.
- The WAAC room, as it was called, though not only female members of the WAAC were welcome, but also female nurses from all the various nursing organisations. This was a women-only room, opened in April 1918, having cafe-type small tables and chairs. On the tables were tablecloths, a luxury their male counterparts could only dream of. In this room was also a piano, and by the largest window in the room was a comfortable three-seater sofa.
- A reading room where newspapers were provided, and also somewhere people could write.
- A games room, with draughts and chess sets, dominoes and the like.

At Camp 13, the YMCA had a second and smaller hut establishment, providing a refreshment buffet and bookstall room, as it was called. The 'Refreshment Buffet' consisted of a serving bar the entire length of the room. This quite large room had tables with a mix of chairs or bench-type seats to go with them. It also had a small raised stage-type area with a piano on it.

Camp 11 had a third, even smaller hut establishment: a recreation room, run by eight ladies who lived in the adjoining hut. It provided a library with some 500 books, facilities for banking, and indoor games including billiards. It held weekly concerts on Wednesdays.

It cannot be overemphasised how valuable these refreshment and recreational facilities were to the military and civilian personnel at Kinmel Camp.

St Margaret's Church (the Marble Church), Bodelwyddan
Once Kinmel Camp was properly up and running in the spring of 1915, it soon became closely entwined with the nearby St Margaret's Church (commonly known as the Marble Church) at Bodelwyddan, near St Asaph. Soldiers from Kinmel Camp attended there, some getting married at the church. Many young soldiers from the camp were confirmed there in ceremonies conducted by the Bishop of St Asaph. Sadly, too many soldiers from Kinmel Camp are buried there. Many were helpless victims of the worldwide Spanish flu pandemic of 1918/1919, but some are buried there after accidents, suicides, or other illnesses. Four of the five Canadian soldiers killed as a result of the Kinmel Park Camp riots on 4 and 5 March 1919 are buried there.

St Margaret's Church was erected at the behest and cost of Lady Margaret Willoughby de Broke, the Widow of

Henry Peyto-Verney, 16th Baron Willoughby de Broke. Lady Margaret was the daughter of the local Sir John Williams of Bodelwyddan Castle. When she married into the Willoughby de Broke family she moved away to reside with her husband in Warwickshire. But when he died, Lady Margaret returned to the Bodelwyddan area. She wished this new church to be a fine and fitting memorial to her late husband.

Lady Margaret laid the foundation stone for the Church on 24 July 1856 and it was completed in 1860 at a cost of £60,000, a great deal of money then. Its cost was said to have virtually bankrupted the family. The designer of it was John Gibson, who had for a time studied with Sir Charles Barry, especially famous for his rebuilding of the Houses of Parliament after the terrible fire of 1834. John Gibson included ornate Gothic carvings to decorate the new church's exterior, which was probably influenced by his time with Sir Charles Barry.

In the churchyard are 111 military burials, with a special memorial to commemorate a further four who were buried at St Peter's Church, Holywell, Flintshire. In relation to Canadian soldiers, there are forty buried in St Margaret's churchyard from deaths that occurred in and around Kinmel Camp in 1918; the remaining Canadian military burials are from 1919.

A Call for Aliens to be Interned at Kinmel Park Camp
In the House of Commons on Thursday, 10 June 1915, during a Question Session, Colonel Hall Walker asked the Home Secretary if he would communicate with his cabinet colleague, the Secretary for War, with the object of taking over the encampment of over 40,000 troops at Kinmel Park, Abergele. So that immediate accommodation could be found at the camp for the Aliens still at large in Britain.

Kinmel Park Camp – Further Developments

By late July 1915, it was reported in the local press that there had been a tremendous influx of new workmen into the district from various parts of the country and as a consequence the work at Kinmel Camp was progressing apace and with more vigour than ever. The Camp was now being fully developed, to be much more than just accommodation for the thousands of soldiers already quartered there. Fresh drafts of soldiers were arriving on a daily basis from the more temporary canvas camps such as the one at Gwenigron, outside St Asaph, which acted as a sort of 'halting ground' for the various battalions until the required amount of hut accommodation became available at Kinmel Camp.

It was now realised locally that the Kinmel Park Military Camp was to be permanent for the foreseeable future. As a result, businesses began to be set up in the vicinity of the camp. Branches of the London City and Midland Bank and the National Provincial Bank had been opened at Tai Newydd, plus premises for cinema shows were about to be erected close by. It was said, 'that the most enterprising among the businessmen and tradesmen of Rhyl were contemplating opening establishments there'. The formerly small hamlet of Kinmel in a very short period of time was developing into one of the most populated places in the whole of north Wales.

Drafts of Soldiers off to the Front

In the first week of August 1915, a draft of some sixteen to twenty soldiers belonging to 16th Battalion, the Royal Welch Fusiliers from Kinmel Camp, made their way on a Wednesday evening to Pensarn station en route to 'the firing line', as it was put in the local press. A tremendous crowd of local residents and visitors to the area congregated to see them off and enthusiastic scenes prevailed. Prominent among those leaving to go to war was a Mexican/Spanish soldier who was said to have brilliant linguistic abilities. Research reveals that he was a private who was Mexican-born, spoke Spanish as his first language and that had travelled the world widely. He was said to have had 'eastern features and served as a Private in the Royal Welch Fusiliers'.

By mid-August 1915, it was reported that due to the recent heavy traction engine traffic to and from Kinmel Camp, serious damage had been caused to the road between Pensarn railway station and the urban boundary with the Rhuddlan Road. The total cost of the repair work was £593.

Officiating Minister Appointed
The Reverend W. G. Owen, the popular pastor of the Abergele and Llanddulas Baptist Churches had been appointed as the Officiating Minister to the Welsh Troops at Kinmel Camp. This announcement was made in a number of the local newspapers. William Griffith Owen was born in 1857 at Pantglas, then in Caernarvonshire, and was by all accounts a popular and well respected Baptist Minister. In 1911, he, his Wife, Lily Adah Owen (nee Jones) and their four children were living on St George's Road, Abergele.

He was better known to many in Wales, especially in Eisteddfodic circles by his bardic name of *Llifon*. He was not only a Baptist minister and army chaplain, but also a poet and excellent Eisteddfod conductor. One of his poems was an elegy to the late R.G. Pritchard of Garreg Wen, Penygroes, near Caernarfon. His Brothers, Alafon and Geraint were also poets. William Griffith (W. G.) Owen died in 1922, aged sixty-five.

More Drafts of Soldiers Leave for the Front

A local newspaper reported in late August of 1915:

> Delightful band music broke the stillness of the night at 1.00 a.m. on Saturday last at Abergele. It was played by the splendid band of the Welsh Regiment from Kinmel Camp, marching to the railway station at the head of a draft of Royal Welsh Fusiliers who were leaving to go to the Western Front. A large number of civilians accompanied the men to the station. Then as their train steamed out of the station, the musicians played in what appeared to the onlookers as a spontaneous gesture Auld Lang Syne.

The soldiers going out in this draft would have been sent to the Western Front and likely been involved in the hell that occurred in late September 1915, 'the Battle of Loos'.

Draft to the Front – a Splendid Presentation given to each Soldier

A draft of some 100 men from 12th (Reserve) Battalion, the Royal Welch Fusiliers, had left Kinmel Camp for the war zone on a Sunday night. Their Commanding Officer had made a splendid presentation to each of the men. On the following Wednesday a further draft of twenty soldiers had left the camp for the Front.

A Weary Walk

Local newspapers reported that on 19 February 1916, local residents had seen the sad sight of some twenty wounded soldiers, some of them being described as having been severely broken in the war, being marched from Pensarn railway station to Kinmel Camp. Their 'four-mile tramp' caused considerable comment in the area. It was said that these poor weary individuals had to stop to rest on occasions and that tears were welling up in their eyes as they went past locals. It was being questioned as to why those in charge did not ask for 'these gallant men to be given transport'; if a request had been made, then a local car or motor vehicle proprietor would have transported the men for free.

2

Life at Kinmel Park Camp

The Photographers of Kinmel Park Camp and its Soldiers
During the Great War it became very popular for British
military service personnel to have their photographs taken
in their respective uniforms as keepsakes to give to their
loved ones or perhaps to be kept for themselves as
mementos. Of course, many had these photographs taken
and gave them to loved ones who never saw them again, and
these photographs became treasured possessions, virtually
family icons, to be shown to the children and grandchildren
of the deceased soldier (serviceman), many of whom had
never seen their fathers.

The soldiers at Kinmel Camp were photographed in
their uniforms either in or around the camp, or in
photographic studios in the nearby towns, particularly in
nearby Rhyl, a popular seaside town where several
photographers and their studios were located.

Two photographers, both with Rhyl-based studios, were
the main producers of such photographs: Rae Pickard's
Portrait Studio and John Williams' Portland Studio. There
was a third, with the rather grand-sounding name of
'American Galleries', who had photographic studios at 7,
Lime Street, Liverpool; 259, Argyle Street, Glasgow and a
probably more temporary studio at 17, High Street, Rhyl,
from where they had a presence at Kinmel Camp. American
Galleries produced a number of posed photographs of
Kinmel Camp-based soldiers in the form of postcards and
ordinary photographs.

In 1915, Rae Pickard's Portrait Studio branched out into
producing photographic postcards of features of the north

Wales coast area, including promenade scenes, churches and general landscapes. He was prolific in producing these, for which we are most grateful as they are a pictorial record of what places and buildings looked like during the Great War and right through into the 1930s.

But once Kinmel Camp was up and running another excellent line of business for Rae Pickard's Portrait Studio was the taking of photographs of soldiers stationed at the camp. Informal type individual and group photographs were taken in and around the camp, with more formal ones being taken back at their Queen Street Studio in Rhyl. Many of these photographs were made into postcards to be sent, handed out or kept by the soldier buyer. Rae Pickard's Portrait Studio also produced a series of photographic postcards entitled 'Somewhere in Kinmel Park'. These scenes taken inside the camp grounds and some even inside the wooden barrack huts, provide us today with a glimpse of what the camp actually looked like in that period.

John Williams first appeared as a photographer, certainly in the Rhyl area in 1895, with premises at 8a, High Street, Rhyl. By 1907, John Williams had moved to premises at 23, High Street, Rhyl and was working under the business name of the 'Portland Studio'. Under the name Jno (a popular spelling of John at the time, especially for business people) Williams, Portland Studio, Rhyl, he began, along with his photographer wife, to take photographs of soldiers and other personnel stationed at the nearby Kinmel Camp. In 1917, he had a small photographic studio at the camp itself. He also continued to take more formal photographs of soldiers and of holidaymakers, using 'artistic backgrounds' at his Portland Studio on High Street, Rhyl. Today you will still come across these photographs in family photograph albums, archives and occasionally for sale on on-line auction sites.

Other photographers who ventured to Kinmel Camp and who took 'outdoor, action-type photographs' of the soldiers stationed there, included A. G. Neshitt, Artist, St Asaph, and J. Wills Jones, Magnet Studio, High Street, Rhyl.

Henry Woolley's Diary of 'His War'

Henry Woolley was born in Aberkenfig, near Bridgend in south Wales. Though he was in a reserved occupation (coal miner hewer), he chose to volunteer, enlisting at Bridgend on 19 January 1915, in 12th Battalion, the Welsh Regiment. He was twenty-six, and lived in Aberkenfig with his wife and two daughters. He was sent for his initial military training to Kinmel Camp. Happily for us today, he kept a diary of his time serving in the Army during the First World War.

When the time came from him to leave Kinmel Camp and be sent out for active service he made this rather poignant entry in his diary:

> I left Kinmel Park August 28th, 11.00 pm, on the way for active service on Gallipoli Peninsula. We fell in on the parade ground the O.C. come round and took the hand of every man, and wished them the best of luck with tears in his eyes, he was more like a father than O.C. He asked every one of us to have a bit of our own back for one of the Captains of the 12th Battalion that had been killed in the Dardanelles a few days before and we told him we would do our best.

Henry Woolley managed to survive the carnage of the War, returning to live the remainder of his life in the Aberkenfig locality.

A Carter Injured

In late August 1915, a carter named Pryce Hughes who lived

at New Street, Abergele, had a narrow escape on a Monday morning when he was driving two spirited horses belonging to Messrs. Richards (W. Alban Richards & Company) who were contractors at Kinmel Camp. The horses suddenly bolted and Pryce Hughes, who hung onto their reins, was pulled onto the ground and suffered injuries. He was removed to the Alexandra Hospital at nearby Rhyl and was subsequently found to have a fractured thigh and extensive bruising.

Schoolboys 'Called Up to Serve' at Kinmel Park Camp!

Bodelwyddan News
BOYS COMMANDEERED FOR SERVICE
A discussion took place at the Rhyl District Schools Committee on the subject of boys being commandeered from the Bodelwyddan School for service as telegraph messengers for the Kinmel Camp.

The attendance officer reported that a post office official attended at the school and took three boys to carry messages to and from the camp.

The members expressed surprise at this and the opinion was expressed that the post official had no power to do such a thing unless acting under military order. If a competent military authority took the boys for military service then the school grant in respect of the boys would not be lost, but in the absence of any such authority the school would suffer.

It was decided that the Director of Education should ascertain under whose orders the boys were commandeered.

Denbighshire Free Press, 11 September 1915

The Red Lion, an Unusual 'Pub', is to Open for Business

ABERGELE

The Red Lion – many years ago this quaint hotel in Bridge Street was referred for compensation on account of redundancy of pubs in the immediate vicinity. Some time afterwards it was bought by the Gas Company, but it remained closed ever since the licence 'went to the dogs'. It has been taken over by the YMCA who intend converting it into a place of amusement, particularly catering for those from the nearby Kinmel Camp.

Denbighshire Free Press, 25 September 1915

The YMCA did indeed open and run the Red Lion, Bridge Street, Abergele, as a 'pub' that served non-alcoholic refreshments and provided recreational facilities to soldiers, particularly those from the nearby Kinmel Park Camp.

Cambridge University and Kinmel Park Camp

In July 1915, Queen's College, Cambridge, funded a YMCA Hut in the camp, staffed during that summer and early autumn by students from Queen's College. In early October 1915, a function was held in honour of the students before they returned to their studies. The Dean, Reverend C. T. Wood, who acted as Superintendent, said of the students: 'They all worked strenuously for the social and spiritual welfare of the Welsh Troops.' Until the next term holidays the Hut would be run by the Hon. Mrs Brodrick and Miss Brodrick.

A Fire in a Hut at Kinmel Park Camp

At about 2.30 am on Friday 8 October 1915 the alarm was sounded throughout the camp, and in just a few minutes every one of the camp's own fire brigade turned out. A fire had broken out in the officers' mess in No. 7 camp, home of 9th Battalion, the South Wales Borderers. Fine work prevented the fire from spreading, despite the strong breeze that was blowing across the camp. The officers' mess was completely gutted and nothing could be saved. Among the items lost were some valuable pictures, the property of one of the officers. Until their mess was rebuilt the officers used the officers' mess in No. 6 camp.

Undesirable Women in and around the Camp!
In mid-October 1915, the local papers got wind of a scandal that was brewing relating to Kinmel Camp. 'Undesirable women' and girls were spending their nights at or in the near vicinity of the camp. One woman from nearby Rhyl, whose husband was at the camp, had deserted her six children in order to be with her husband at the camp. For this, the woman subsequently received from the Rhyl magistrates the prison sentence of three months' imprisonment with hard labour. Her six children were sent to the local workhouse. This case was said to have been the first prosecution taken in the 'Union' under the provisions of the Prevention of Cruelty to Children Act, 1908. This gave the powers to hand down a sentence of up to two years imprisonment.

Further investigations into the whole matter of the 'undesirable women' revealed that a number of women were spending their nights either in the woods that adjoined the camp, or in some of the unfinished huts inside the camp itself. The vast majority of these women most certainly had no family connections with any of the soldiers or civilians at the camp, but were in fact 'ladies of the night'.

In late October 1915, further problems occurred of 'undesirable women' frequenting Kinmel Camp at night. The garrison military police, under the orders of the assistant provost marshal, were said to be active in stopping 'the mischief', as were the local police. These 'ladies' were now also frequenting the roads around the camp.

In mid-November 1915, the issue of the 'undesirable women', women who were obviously desirable to some at Kinmel Camp, had become something of a cause celebre. The Chief Constable reported to the local council that his men were doing their best to sort out the problem. The woods around the Kinmel Park Estate and the camp had never seen such a hive of human (rather than animal) activity before. By the following week this 'undesirable women' problem was taking on epic proportions. Police Superintendent Beresford reported that 'the evil was not as bad as it was, as a large number of Civil Guards from the Volunteer Training Corps had been sworn in as Special Constables and were involved in the matter'.

Recruiting for the Welsh Guards

On Thursday 26 November 1915, Lord Harlech, Colonel of the Welsh Guards, visited Kinmel Camp as part of a special recruiting tour for that fine, then quite newly-formed regiment. He intimated that 'Men who have joined other units have the privilege of transferring to the Welsh Guards, the eligibility being for those of Welsh parentage, or language, or otherwise being associated with Wales. The minimum height requirement being 5 feet 7 inches.'

Lord Harlech was accompanied by General Sir Owen Thomas and it was said that from the two Welsh battalions at the camp at this time, there was 'An immediate and gratifying response to their appeal'.

Persons Wanted at Kinmel Park Camp

The *Liverpool Echo* of Friday, 24 December 1915, had this piece on its front page relating to Kinmel Camp under the heading of 'Persons Wanted':

BLACKSMITHS' Strikers,
at once, several, good; 7d per hour:
4th Army Camp, Rhyl.
(Telephone 48 Abergele).

Everyday Matters at Kinmel Park Camp

Milk dealers supplying the large amounts of milk daily to Kinmel Camp were told that they were required to register and for their cowsheds to be in 'proper order' before any more milk was supplied by them to the camp.

More than 3,000 parcels had been delivered to Kinmel Camp during the Christmas and New Year period, in addition to many thousands of letters. No fewer than 700 being registered items. Plus 14,000 telegrams had passed through the camp Post Office over the yuletide period. To assist Mr Williams, the Chief Officer of the Military Post Office, and his permanent civilian staff at Kinmel Camp with the heavy workload, they had been assisted by some soldiers from the camp during the holiday period.

About the Coldest Place I have ever been in!

The *Koroit Sentinel and Tower Hill Advocate*, Victoria, Australia, had a very candid account of life at Kinmel Camp from one of our Antipodean Cousins:

Personal
Private William Baxter, of the Royal Welsh Fusiliers, writes from Kinmel Park, Rhyl, north Wales, dated 31 December, as follows: north Wales is about the coldest place I have ever been in. We are camped right along the foot of a range of mountains and north Wales is noted for its weather. For four weeks, without a break hardly, we have had snow every day. This camp is only a new one and in various ways is not

completed yet, so we are not comfortable by any means. I cannot say it has had a bad effect on me. In fact it is just the reverse and I am doing well on it – all day in the open agrees with me O.K.

I have just returned from a week's leave in London, and the first night I was there the Zeppelins appeared. They seem to have a set on me for sure as I go near London they come to light. But their day is done. London will not be troubled with many more of them for they have had too warm a reception. The war seems to be no nearer the end, in fact the longer it lasts the worse it gets. I am a soldier now after four month's training, and some shot too, being attached to the snipers' corps. I had to go to Aldershot (which is the largest military camp in the world, and the most modern) to do a musketry course, and qualified as a marksman scoring 169 points out of 180. Not a bad performance, but four months in the open air has made a wonderful difference to me in health. The Welsh people of course have a language of their own, which makes it fairly hard to understand them. The front is a place I may see before this reaches you. Part of our first battalion are now in Salonika, and our crowd will act as a reserve battalion here to fill up the gaps. That is the disadvantage of a reserve battalion, who do not go out all together, but in drafts of two or three hundred at a time, which means very often that you get separated from your pals. Nothing upsets a soldier more than to get into a strange company. I have not got the stripes up yet and don't intend to if I can help it. In the English army you have by far the best time in the ranks, and you do not get paid anything extra as a lance-corporal, corporal or a sergeant, until you have done three months' service with the stripes on.

Koroit Sentinel and Tower Hill Advocate,
Saturday 19 February 1916

Preaching in Uniform

In the second week of January 1916, Army Chaplain John Williams from Kinmel Camp preached in uniform at Capel Mawr, Denbigh, north Wales. He was known in the Welsh-speaking community as 'Wilias Brynsiencyn', having come from Brynsiencyn on Anglesey.

A Lonely Heart

In the second week of January 1916, an advert had been placed in a local newspaper from a 28-year-old single army sergeant, presently convalescing at Kinmel Camp, stating that he wished to meet or correspond with a local young lady. Also that photographs could be exchanged care of the newspaper's editor.

An Appeal for Recruits

In the third week of January 1916 several newspapers, including the *Liverpool Daily Post*, published an appeal by Colonel T. A. Wynne-Edwards for recruits. He was at the time the Commanding Officer of 21st Battalion, the Royal Welch Fusiliers stationed at Kinmel Camp. This battalion acted as one of the 'feeder battalions' supplying drafts of soldiers to the Service Battalion. He also announced that a University Company would be included in 21st Battalion.

Officer Cadet Units

In February 1916, a new system of training officers for the British Army was introduced. From now on Temporary

Commissions could only be given to a soldier if he had been through an Officer Cadet Training Unit. The entrant was required to be aged over eighteen and a half and to have already served in the ranks and been recommended by his Commanding Officer, or had previous officer experience, or had a specialist qualification. The training course lasted eighteen weeks, at the end of which an examination was required to be passed. The training courses were said to have been designed to develop leadership skills, encourage initiative and to try to instil self-confidence. An Officer Cadet Battalion was to have an establishment at any one time of 400 cadets, though this was raised to 600 in May of 1917, if a particular unit could accommodate them. In total some 73,000 men gained Infantry Commissions after being trained in such Officer Cadet Battalions. As the war progressed more and more of these came straight from the ranks. At Kinmel Camp two such Officer Training Battalions operated, namely O.T.B. Number 16 and O.T.B. Number 17.

Worship Followed by Innocent Entertainment
Consequent upon the arrival of many hundreds of Welsh-speaking soldiers at Kinmel Camp, the attendance at the various places of worship in the locality on Sunday evenings greatly increased. As a result schoolrooms were being opened to entertain the men after the services had finished, which the soldiers were said to have greatly appreciated.

Billiards Match

A Billiards Match took place between The Conservative Club, Denbigh and the Sergeant's Mess of the 9th Battalion, the South Wales Borderers, Kinmel Park.

Denbighshire Free Press, 26 February 1916

Military Parade Abandoned

In consequence of the adverse weather conditions, the St David's Day (1 March 1916) parade through Abergele from Kinmel Camp was abandoned. Flags had been displayed in Abergele by locals for the St David's Day Parade.

Jewish Soldiers from South Wales

The *Aberdare Leader* of 3 March 1916 carried this story:

> JEWISH BOYS WITH THE FORCES
> On Monday Mr Solomon Silverman, Aberdare, left to join the 2nd Monmouthshire Regiment. Other local Jewish young men already in the Army are: Private Arthur Jacobs, 11th Welsh, Salonica; Private Nat. Robins, Aberaman, 13th Welsh, Rhyl; Private Eli Bloch, 1st Mons; and the Bros. Mark and Alec Abelsom, with the same regiment at Bedford; Private Mossie Goldstone, Royal Welsh Fusiliers, Kinmel Park; Private Hyman Levinson (formerly of Jacob's, Cardiff Street), with the 3rd Mons., stationed at Oswestry; Private Lewis Corb, Mountain Ash, with the 1st Mons. At Bedford.

The two Jewish soldiers mentioned in the article who were at the time stationed at Kinmel Camp were Private Nat Robins and Private Mossie Goldstone. Nat Robins was Nathan Robins, born 18 October 1892 at Pontypool. He was a son of Russian-born parents, Simon Robins, a furniture dealer, and his wife, Gertrude – almost certainly anglicised names were assumed by the couple when coming to Britain. In 1901 and still in 1911, the Robins family resided at 191, Cardiff Road, Aberaman, Aberdare, Glamorgan.

On 2 February 1916, Nat Robins attested and enlisted in the Welsh Regiment. He was a single man, and gave his home address as 13, Lewis Street, Aberaman, Aberdare, and his occupation as furniture dealer. Nat Robins was posted to 12th (Reserve) Battalion for his initial military training to take place at Kinmel Camp. Whilst there he fell foul of the military authorities on three separate occasions. On 29 May 1916, he was absent from Kinmel Camp; for this first offence he was confined to barracks for three days. On 6 July 1916 at Kinmel Camp he was again absent and received an official admonishment and forfeited three days' pay. Shortly before leaving the camp he was again absent on 14 August 1916 and for this offence he initially was fined six days' pay, which was later reduced to just the forfeiture of three days' pay. On 30 August 1916, Private Nat Robins now with 11th (Service) Battalion, the Welsh Regiment, embarked from Devonport in a troopship bound for Salonika, Greece.

Private Mossie Goldstone was Mostyn Henry Goldstone, born 19 March 1890, to Russian-born parents, Solomon and Bertha Goldstone, who resided for many years at 84, Cardiff Road, Aberaman, Aberdare. Solomon was a pawnbroker in 1901, but by 1911 he was a furniture dealer. Solomon and Bertha had had eight children by 1911, but in this year only three were still alive, including Mostyn Henry, who was known by friends and fellow soldiers as 'Mossie'. Mossie Goldstone was transferred to the Liverpool Regiment and became an Acting Sergeant. He was later again transferred, this time to the Labour Corps, Corps Number 49810. He survived the War and subsequently received the Victory and British War Medals.

Allegations of Bullying at Kinmel Camp – an Attempted Suicide

Preferred Death To Military Service
At a Special Court held on Friday last, allegations of

Kinmel Park Camp, between the hutments

Inside one of the huts

Portrait of an unknown soldier taken inside the photographic hut just outside Kinmel Park Camp

Private Robert Owen, 20th Battalion, RWF, who died of illness on 1st April, 1916

The grave in Mallwyd of Private Robert Owen – he was buried with his father, David Owen

Gravestone of Lt Arthur Lloyd, Birkenhead (Flaybrick Hill) Cemetery

The bandstand inside Kinmel Camp

The main entrance to Kinmel Camp, c. 1916

An officers' hockey team

A Kinmel Park Camp postcard, posted in 1916

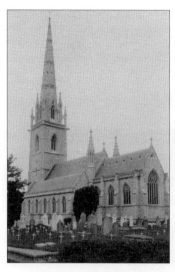

St Margaret's church and churchyard, 'the Marble Church', Bodelwyddan after WW1, with military crosses in the foreground

Soldier on horseback at Kinmel Camp

J. B. Priestley as a young soldier, c.1915; he later underwent officer training at Kinmel Camp

George John Culpitt, probably taken at Kinmel Park Camp

The YMCA hut at No. 13 Camp, Kinmel Park Camp

*Interior of the above hut, showing the refreshment counter
and inside the YMCA hut – lengthways view*

The YMCA Central Pavilion at No. 4 Camp, Kinmel Camp

The YMCA Central Pavilion, No. 4 Camp
– the cinema and concert hall

*Robert Graves in uniform
during WW1*

*Gravestone of J. V. Hawkins, shot
dead by John Jenner at Kinmel
Park Camp on 1 May, 1918.*

*Lance-Sergeant Leonard Nuttall,
who sadly committed suicide*

*Lt Stanley Henry Parry Boughey
V.C., killed in action
on 4 December 1917*

The WAACs' room – 'women only' –
Central Pavilion, No. 4 Camp, c.1918

Post Office staff, c.1916

The billiard room in the YMCA Central Pavilion. No. 4 Camp

Field Marshall Sir John French's visit to Kinmel Camp in 1916

Party of Royal Engineers working on the Kinmel Camp Railway c.1915-17

William Griffith Owen, 'Llifon',
Officiating Minister at
Kinmel Park Camp

Thomas Jones, South Wales
Borderers, who was from Groes,
near Denbigh

The Albert Medal awarded
to Lt Albert Nevitt

Peace Medal of the Royal Welch Fusiliers, c.1919

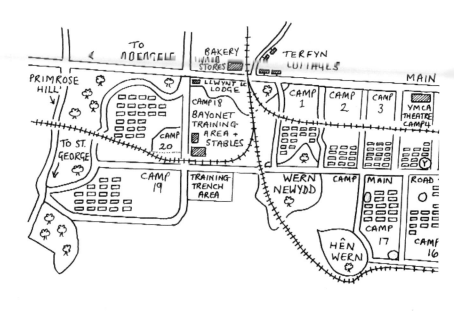

@	QUARTERMASTER'S STORES AREA
Y	Y.M.C.A.
NACB	NAVY, ARMY + CANTEEN BOARD CENTRAL STORES
LC	LEVEL CROSSING
+++++++	RAILWAY
◯	POND
🌳	WOODED AREA

KINMEL PARK CAMP
1915-1918

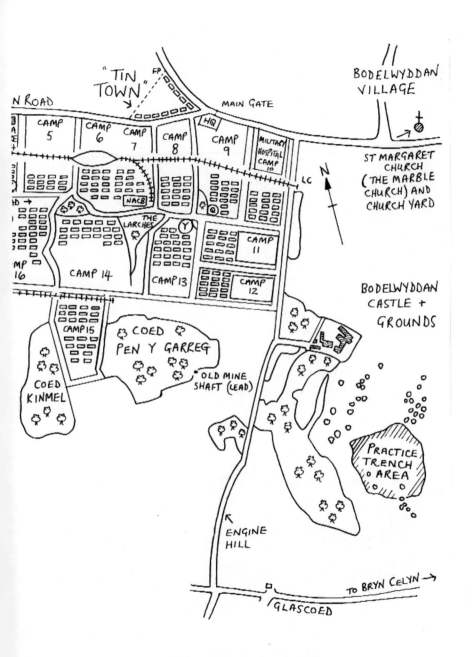

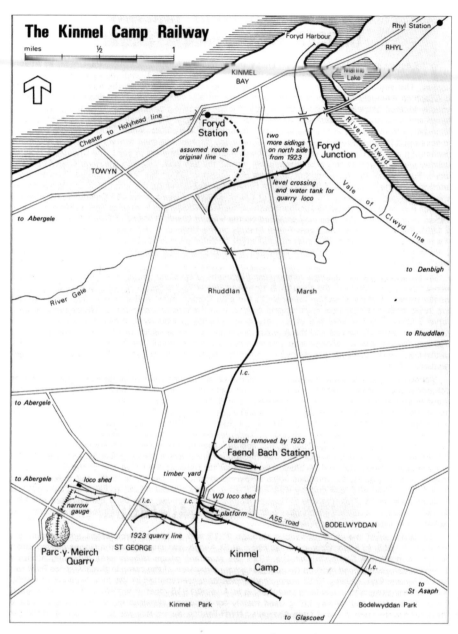

The Kinmel Camp Railway (the KCR)

bullying at Kinmel Camp were made. Before the court was Private William Hope of the 14th Battalion, the South Wales Borderers, presently stationed at Kinmel Camp. Private Hope pleaded guilty to arranging to commit suicide by throwing himself off the Rhuddlan Bridge into the River Clwyd. He had only joined the Army two days earlier, being a Conscript and on his way back to the camp after a march, he jumped into the river and although there was a depth of fifteen feet, he did not sink.

Sgt. Bradley of the gymnasium staff was passing at the time and he rescued the man, then working for some time to restore animation. Private Hope said that he was afraid of some of the men and that one had threatened to cut off his head. He was sorry for what he had done and would not do it again. He did not want to join the Army but was forced to. In discharging the man on his own recognisance the Magistrates appealed to Hope to do his best to make a good soldier and if he wanted to die, to do so facing the foe. At the same time the Magistrates asked the officers to do their best to stop the bullying of recruits at the camp, as they themselves had heard something about it. Lieutenant Lloyd who was in Court said he would look after the man but had heard no complaint of bullying such as the man had now made.

Route March to St Asaph
The local newspapers reported that on Wednesday, 29 March 1916, a very large number of soldiers from Kinmel Camp had a route march to the city of St Asaph and then back to the camp. An observer proffered, that considering the weather had been so cold and wet, the men looked well. Though it reached the newspapers that several soldiers had

complained of colds in the camp, but that was not a surprise as the weather had been so foul of late. It was further reported that amongst many others, Mr John Hughes a local draper, a son of the late Reverend B. Hughes, would be leaving Kinmel Camp for the Front at the end of the week.

Not only Military Training for Soldiers at Kinmel Park Camp

The *Aberdare Leader* of 8 April 1916, carried this story in relation to the extracurricular activities of soldiers stationed at Kinmel Camp:

> **Abercwmboi News**
> Pte. D. T. Evans, 21st RWF, who is stationed at Kinmel Camp, Abergele, son of Mr and Mrs Thomas Evans of 64, John Street, is making a name in the musical world. A military choir under Pte. Evans' direction took part in a concert held on St David's Day at Kinmel Park. On Monday week at The Pavillion, Rhyl, Pte. Evans gave two violin solos. Also his Male Voice Party picked from the 21st sang. This Party has entered for the Male Voice Choir competition at the Easter Monday Eisteddfod at Mold.

Cultivation Scheme for the Camp

In the second week of April 1916, a scheme had begun at Kinmel Camp for the cultivation of the vacant plots of ground around 'the hutments' for the purpose of helping the national economy and also to beautify the place for the benefit of the soldiers stationed there. A request was made locally for anyone wishing to assist this scheme to do so by sending flowers and vegetables of all kinds to Lieutenant R. E. West, 21st Battalion, the Royal Welch Fusiliers, No. 12 Camp, Kinmel Camp.

Wesleyan Methodist Institute Opening
The opening of the Wesleyan Institute at Kinmel Camp took place on 6 April 1916. It was officially opened in a short ceremony conducted by Lieutenant-Colonel Owen Thomas (later to become Brigadier-General Sir Owen Thomas MP).

A Real Mystery and one that Remains so to the Present Time
The *Liverpool Echo* of Thursday 20 April 1916, carried this rather intriguing little piece:

> **Solicitor and Soldier**
> Mr Haydn Jones has given notice to ask the Under Secretary for War if he will state what circumstances Mr T. Forcer Evans, Solicitor, of Holyhead, now a Private in the 2nd Royal Welsh Fusiliers, has been requested to be sent to Wrexham, under an escort. What is the charge against Mr Evans and under what circumstances the authorities at Wrexham exercise control over the Military at Kinmel Park Camp?

No explanation has been found to date!

An Amazing Effort to Enlist
The Saturday 22 April 1916 edition of *The Kalgoorlie (Australia) Miner* carried this short piece:

> An overseas Englishman who travelled 2,000 miles by train and 4,000 miles by sea in order to enlist in the British Army was rejected as unfit on his arrival in England. War work has now been found for him at Kinmel Camp.

Abergele Entertainments Committee

The local newspapers in early May of 1916 reported that during the winter (of 1915) the Abergele Entertainments Committee had regularly given concerts in the various separate camps that made up Kinmel Camp.

Soldier Volunteers Working in the Hayfields

In the second week of June 1916, the local newspapers were carrying the story that over 400 men from the Kinmel Park Convalescent Camp had answered the call for volunteers to work in the hayfields. The men were to be sent to Chester in one draft to carry out the work.

A 'Truly Glorious Send-off'

In the third week of June 1916, the first draft of soldiers from 21st and 22nd Battalions of the Royal Welch Fusiliers stationed at Kinmel Camp left the camp for the Front. They were travelling on the Friday evening's 8.24 p.m. train from Abergele/Pensarn railway station. According to a local newspaper account:

> They were headed by a silver band and whatever fate has in store for these gallant lads, they will never forget the truly glorious send-off the Abergele people gave them. Hundreds of people followed the Welsh 'Tommies' to the station. Although the parting was sad and painful enough, it was an inspiring moment for everybody present. They sang 'Rhondda' and 'Hyfrydol' on the station platform, with stirring fervour. As the train moved off, the thunderous cheering of the multitude and the playing of 'Auld Lang Syne' by the band, was a magnificent finale to a very eventful evening. It appears that the men have already landed safely 'somewhere in France'.

A postcard was received from a Private Tom R. Jones some weeks later, stating that this draft of soldiers had landed safely in France after having a good time en route.

Concert to be given at Mumbles
Llais Llafur – Labour Voice of 8 July 1916 had this advertisement for a concert:

MUMBLES PIER & PAVILION
Sunday, July 9th at 3.45 p.m. and 6.45 p.m.
THE POPULAR BAND OF THE 21st BATTALION,
THE WELSH REGIMENT.
(Kinmel Park, Rhyl) Conductor – Mr Jas. Roberts.

The accounts needed to be balanced!
In mid-July of 1916, it was reported that some forty London City and Midland Bank clerks in training at Kinmel Camp had been sent back temporarily to their former bank premises to assist with the half-yearly balancing of the accounts. They were then required to return to military duty at Kinmel Camp by no later than the following weekend.

The London City and Midland Bank established a small branch at Tai Newydd, near to Kinmel Camp. The London City and Midland Bank had been founded in August of 1836, by Charles Geach, formerly of the Bank of England. He obtained financial support for his new bank, particularly from business backers in the Birmingham area. It was founded as the Birmingham and Midland Bank. The bank expanded rapidly in the Midlands, absorbing many of the local independent banks, until in 1891, it merged with the Central Bank of London. This entity became known as the London City and Midland Bank from 1891 until 1923. In 1923 after expanding throughout the country and making further acquisitions, it adopted the new name of the

Midland Bank, a title it kept until it became part of HSBC Bank Plc.

Marriage at Aberdaron of a Kinmel Park Camp Soldier
This extract is taken from an account of the wedding of a soldier based at Kinmel Camp, to a young lady from Aberdaron in Llŷn, which appeared in the 28 July 1916 edition of the *Cambrian News and Merionethshire Standard*:

> ABERDARON
> WEDDING – On Thursday of last week, at St Hywyn Parish, the marriage was solemnized between Private R. H. D. Keeling, 22nd Welsh Regiment, Kinmel Park, and of The Burghe, Market Drayton, Salop, and Miss May Josephine Armstrong, of Carrog, Aberdaron, and Wexford.

Visit of Mr David Lloyd George to Kinmel Park Camp
On 20 August 1916, David Lloyd George made an 'official' visit to Kinmel Camp. From May 1915 until early July 1916, Lloyd George had been the Minister of Munitions. However, upon the death of Lord Kitchener (drowned at sea en route to Russia) he had from 6 July 1916 been appointed as Secretary of State for War.

Lloyd George was present for the first service to be held in the newly built Interdenominational Hut for the soldiers stationed there. The term 'hut' for this building is rather misleading as it could hold up to 1,000 worshippers. It had been provided by four Nonconformist bodies – the Calvinists, Methodists, Baptists and Congregationalists. David Lloyd George spoke to the throng in both English and Welsh of national unity, even though people may not share the same religious beliefs. That there could be unity of purpose and action, but that would not presuppose unity of faith and unity of creed in all matters relating to the people. He pleaded for unity among and tolerance of, all religions, and went on to say that one of the first things he did when appointed as Secretary of State for War was to set up an Interdenominational Committee in the War Office, to advise him and the Army Council as to the best way of making religious arrangements, carried out so as to suit the exigencies of the new great National Army, the sheer size of which, the country had never seen before.

Less than four months after this visit to Kinmel Camp, David Lloyd George became Prime Minister in December 1916, succeeding Herbert Asquith. He remained Prime Minister for the remainder of the First World War and indeed until 1922, leading a Coalition Government.

A Concert to be Given

This advertisement for a Concert appeared in *Llais Llafur – Labour Voice* of 2 September 1916. Mumbles (also known as Oystermouth) is a seaside town near Swansea, south Wales:

MUMBLES PIER & PAVILION
Sunday, September 3rd, at 3.45 p.m. and 6.45 p.m.
The Band 3rd Batt. South Wales Borderers.
(4th Gwent) KINMEL PARK.

The Closure of a Road at Night for Safety Reasons

In early September 1916, owing to the high number of accidents on the roads to Bodelwyddan and Kinmel Camp, which stood, according to the *Denbighshire Free Press* of Saturday, 2 September 1916, at five soldiers killed, seven seriously injured and thirteen injured, a meeting was held. As a result, after consultation between the Local Authority and Brigadier-General Dunn of Kinmel Camp, it was decided to close the Bodelwyddan Road and Ty Fry Road to motor cars between the hours of sunset and sunrise during the winter months.

How Dare Ordinary People Live above their Menns and Stations in Life!
This lighter story, laced with the elitism and sexism of the day, appeared in the *Liverpool Echo* edition of Saturday 23 September 1916:

WASHERWOMEN IN MOTOR-CARS.
At the Rhyl County Court, two washerwomen, of St Asaph, were sued for the hire of motor-cars. In one case the debt was £2, and in the second £9.

The Registrar: What do washerwomen want with motor-cars?
Plaintiff: They go to Kinmel with washing. [Laughter in the Court]
Mr Gamlin: Washerwomen are making a lot of money at the camp?
(Plaintiff's Solicitor)
Plaintiff: Yes, I have seen them draw £25 a month.
Mr Gamlin: But why did you let a woman run up a debt of £9?
Plaintiff: It was for a wedding trip. The daughter was married, and then the party went for a motor trip to Chester and Liverpool. [Laughter again in the Court]
Mr Gamlin: Did the daughter marry a private soldier or an officer?
Plaintiff: A private.

Mr Gamlin:	What was he in private life?
Plaintiff:	A postman.
Mr Gamlin:	Yet he went for a wedding motor trip to Liverpool?
Plaintiff:	Yes. [Laughter again in the Court]

The Registrar made substantial orders in each case.

Special Concession given to Soldiers from Kinmel Park Camp

In the first week of October 1916, it was announced in the local newspapers that a special concession was to be given to soldiers from Kinmel Camp. The toll charge at the Foryd Bridge, Rhyl, would be half-price for them.

Buildings are Going Up Everywhere!

Mr F Bibby JP presided over a [council] meeting to consider the problem of illegal building on the outskirts of Kinmel Park Camp. The Sanitary Inspector reported that certain buildings had been put up near the camp in the parish of Bodelwyddan, not in accordance with the plans submitted to the council. The buildings included a hairdresser's shop, chip potato saloon, shops and bungalow. Certain nuisance existed, while a motor garage has been erected without any plan being submitted. He asked for the council's instructions in the matter. Before penalties were imposed it was decided to first communicate with all the parties concerned for an explanation.

Denbighshire Free Press, 28 October 1916

Fanny 4d – Camp Harpie!

In November of 1916, a woman named Fanny Jones, whose home address was said to be in Colwyn Bay, appeared at the Rhyl Police Court. She was charged with 'immoral behaviour at the Kinmel Park Army Camp'. One local newspaper for their brief account of the case had the headline for it as, 'Camp Harpie sent to Prison'. She was sent to prison for one month. The court was informed that the defendant best known as 'Fanny 4d' (fourpence), had three or four previous convictions against her for similar offences. We may draw our own conclusions as to what the nickname 'Fanny 4d' referred, in relation to this 'lady of the night'.

What, Soldiers Drilling on a Sunday and there was no Dinner for Them?

KINMEL PARK CAMP

COMPLAINTS OF DRILLING ON SUNDAYS

Mr William Thorne, in the House of Commons on Monday, asked the Financial Secretary to the War Office if he was aware that on Sunday 3 December a number of men of the 63rd Battalion Training Reserve, stationed at 20th Camp, Kinmel Park, Denbighshire, were paraded and drilled. And that on arrival at the camp were unable to obtain dinner as there was not enough to go around; and whether he would endeavour to stop the practice of strenuous drilling on Sundays, and make enquiries into the alleged lack of food.

Mr Macpherson: I have made inquiry, and I find that the feeding arrangements on the occasion in question were quite satisfactory and that there was no question of any shortage of food. No complaints were received from the orderly officers, nor from any NCO or man on that day. No drilling is done on Sundays beyond what the exigencies of the service require.

North Wales Chronicle, 22 December 1916

Motor Omnibuses
In late December of 1916, Flintshire County Council sanctioned the running of motor omnibuses between Rhyl and Kinmel Camp. This was on condition that a charge of one penny (1d) per mile be paid to the council by the owners and operators of the vehicles for the use of the road. The owners and operators agreed to making the stipulated payments.

A Claim for Compensation
At the Rhyl County Court, Edward Jones, a painter and decorator from the locality claimed compensation at the rate of 18 shillings per week for loss of earnings for an injury he said he had sustained whilst working at Kinmel Camp. He claimed he had fallen off a hut at the camp and had injured his ankle.

Who was the Ass?
In late December of 1916, it was reported that one of the Non-Commissioned Officers based at Kinmel Camp had been walking out of the gates of the camp, when he passed an officer and one of the army mules standing close together. He apparently took no notice of the officer, but this 'Tommy' saluted the mule. For his sublime cheek, indeed insubordination, he was lucky to escape with nothing more than the punishment of being confined to barracks for two days.

An Interrupted Marriage, with no Honeymoon!

An unnamed young soldier in training at Kinmel Camp had made arrangements to get married on a Saturday morning in late December 1916. But his Superior Officer at the camp had declined to grant him a leave of absence. However, the young soldier paid no heed. Instead he took what was called then 'French Leave' from the camp. He felt it was worth going 'Absent Without Leave' (AWOL) as the wedding could not be postponed! He hired a motor car and proceeded with all speed to a location somewhere in Flintshire, where his eager bride-to-be was waiting for him. The army hierarchy at the camp had, however, sent a telegram and by the time this gallant young lad in khaki arrived at the place of worship for his wedding, there was a military escort party waiting to return him to the camp forthwith. The military police took pity on him and were honourable and humane enough to let the wedding ceremony take place, but as soon as it had ended, they took the young private into custody and whisked him sharply away from his bride. In due course, being under arrest, he was returned to Kinmel Camp later the same afternoon and was sent out in a draft of soldiers to India that same night.

Concerts given by Officer Cadet Battalion

In late December 1916 and in early January 1917, 16th Officer Cadet Battalion stationed at Kinmel Camp, held a series of concerts at the camp itself and at suitable venues in nearby Rhyl. Lieutenant-Colonel L.C. Morley presided, with Lieutenant Boughey (Stanley Henry Parry Boughey, later that year to be posthumously awarded the Victoria Cross) and Officer Cadet Roberts being mainly responsible for the arrangements. Amongst the 'delightfully rendered' musical items, as the *Rhyl Journal* put it, were pianoforte sketches by Captain Grierson, songs by Mrs Grierson, songs by Cadet Potter accompanied on the piano and violin by Cadets, Roberts and Munday. Cello solos being given by Cadet Munday, violin solos by Cadet Corsby, whistling solos by Cadet Godwin; humourous turns included those by Cadets Piercey and Davies. Also various selections from Cadets Burke, Wray, Smith and Horder. One of the organisers, Cadet Roberts, proved 'a most efficient accompanist'. Such a success had these concerts been over the Christmas and New Year period that arrangements were said to be well in hand for the formation of a Battalion orchestra and it was hoped that shortly a Battalion choir would also be formed.

Concert given at Kinmel Park Camp

In the second week of January 1917 a musical party from the Carmel Welsh Congregationalist Chapel at Queen Street, Rhyl, gave a concert at the Free Church Institute at Kinmel Camp. A varied programme was given, which, it was said was enjoyed by a crowded house who were in attendance.

Sunday Afternoon Meetings at Kinmel Park Camp

The Reverend E. J. Gruffydd, previously the Pastor of the Bethel Congregational Church, Trecynon, near Aberdare, south Wales, established when there the innovation of a monthly service of song. Then when he was appointed as a Chaplain at Kinmel Camp he organised a PSA Association movement (Pleasant Sunday Afternoon Association) at the camp, providing for the soldiers, within a religious framework, meetings which were interesting in content and that proved to be well-attended. Held every Sunday in the spacious Free Church Hall at Kinmel Camp and under the direction of Reverend E. J. Gruffydd, a musical programme was presented together with thoughtful addresses, talks or lectures. On one occasion Sir Herbert Roberts, MP, delivered to the attenders a 'most timely and instructive address bearing on the capture of Jerusalem', as the *Aberdare Leader* described it.

On occasions the PSA Association at Kinmel Camp would have in attendance 'girls in khaki and a sprinkling of civilians'.

In early January of 1917, with the Free Church Hall full, Chaplain Gruffydd presided over a 'delightful programme for the congregation'. Mr J. Herbert Lewis, MP gave an address on the theme of the capture of Jerusalem and spoke of the successful campaign in the Holy Land of Britain and its Allies in the present War. He also spoke of his own two personal visits in the past to Palestine. A service of song then took place, as was the norm for these meetings.

Military Equipment and Clothing for Sale

In the first weeks of 1917, the *Rhyl Journal* carried this advertisement for a local shop at which I am sure soldiers from Kinmel Camp availed themselves of military equipment and clothing, particularly before they went overseas with a draft from their respective battalions:

> MILITARY EQUIPMENT – THE BON, Corner of High Street and Wellington Road.
> Proprietor: John Brookes.
> Khaki Shirts, Socks, Mufflers, Puttees, Sweaters, Helmets, Handkerchiefs etc.
> Lanyards, Chevrons, Worsted Badges.
> WATERPROOF GOODS: Cap Covers, Trench Seats, 'Bon Westers', Oil Proofed and Rubber Coats, Jackets and Overalls.
> Kit Bags, Haversacks, Caps, Holdalls, Hussifs etc. etc.

Soldiers from Kinmel Park Camp are 'Confirmed'

On Sunday, 10 January 1917, at St Margaret's Church, Bodelwyddan, the Bishop of St Asaph, Alfred George

Edwards, held a confirmation for soldiers. Here 230 young soldiers were in one ceremony 'confirmed' in the Church of England. This was the sixth such ceremony to take place involving young soldiers from Kinmel Camp.

The *Rhyl Journal* stated: 'The Confirmation is always an impressive sight, but never more so than when the candidates are young Men, many of whom are to move out to the Front in a few days.'

A Grand Military Concert

Grand Military Concert
Thursday, January 18th 1917
Church House, St Asaph at 7.30 p.m.
Artistes from Kinmel Camp
Tickets 2s and 1s
Proceeds for St Asaph District Nurse Fund

Train Jumped the Rails
A Kinmel Camp Railway (KCR) locomotive on a journey between Kinmel Camp and Rhyl jumped the metals in crossing the Abergele to St Asaph road on Wednesday evening, 24 January 1917. The mishap resulted in the complete stoppage of vehicular traffic along the thoroughfare for some time. A local motorist was reported in the local press to have succeeded in reaching Abergele by taking his car through the camp and out again at Golden Lodge. So much for the security at Kinmel Camp!

Kinmel Camp Free Church Hall
A Free Church Hall had recently been erected at Kinmel Camp, at the joint expense of the Baptists, Congregationalists and Calvinistic Methodists, each denomination having contributed its share of the total cost of £500.

The Electric Picture Palace, Abergele

In the first week of February 1917, The Electric Picture Palace Cinema at Abergele was sold by its sole proprietor, Mr Edward Simons to 'a Gentleman', Mr John Holroyd of Colwyn Bay. At this time the cinema advertised the 'popular prices of 4d and 7d', with doors open at 7.30 p.m. and the showing of films commencing at 8.00. p.m. Mr Edward Simons had reluctantly to sell the Electric Picture Palace Cinema due to his having been called up for military service. In September of 1917, Mr Edward Simons was reported as being a driver with the Army Service Corps in France.

Fine New Church Army Hut for Kinmel Park Camp

On Friday 2nd February 1917, Colonel Lord Mostyn formally opened the fine new Church Army Hut at Kinmel Camp. The original one, made purely of wood, was 75 feet long by 25 feet wide and was to be used as an annexe in which a 'dry' canteen (no-alcohol served) would be run. The new Church Army Hut for 'the many Church of England soldiers at the camp' was 120 feet in length, built on brick pile, and made of wood and corrugated iron. It was said to be able to accommodate 1,400 people and was coated in a fireproof paint. Many dignitaries were present at this opening including the Countess of Dundonald and Lady Mostyn.

Decorated for their War Service

In February 1917, some female members of staff at the military hospital at Kinmel Camp were 'decorated for their War Service'. These nursing staff included Miss E. St Quintin, Sister and Acting Matron. The military hospital at the camp was said in the press to be, 'a huge institution'. This announcement officially appeared in the *London Gazette Supplement* of 23 February 1917. Miss E. St Quintin was a member of Queen Alexandra's Imperial Military Nursing Service (QAIMNS).

Silver Motor Company Increase Fares

In the third week of April 1917, the local newspapers carried details of an increase in the fares of the Silver Motor Company. The new fares were to be: Kinmel to Abergele Town – 4d for soldiers and 5d for civilians; Kinmel to Abergele station – 4 and a half pence for soldiers and 6d for civilians; Abergele town to the station – now 2d.

The Wonderful Letters of Ida Elizabeth Haigh (later Gould)

On or shortly before 21 April 1917, 24-year-old Ida Elizabeth Haigh arrived at Kinmel Camp to take up the position of a Voluntary Aid Detachment (VAD) nurse. Ida was born on 4 May 1892, in Bradford, Yorkshire, to Stephen Cutt Haigh, a Yorkshire-born textile merchant and his wife, Emma Serine. Prior to Ida's birth her parents had resided in Chorlton-on-Medlock, Lancashire, but by 1901 the family resided at 9, Spring Bank, Bradford.

By 1911, with the family business flourishing, the Haigh family had moved to a larger house at 6, Mornington Villas, Bradford, and had two servants, a cook and a maid. Ida Haigh wished to contribute to the war effort and volunteered for the VAD. Ida Haigh carried out her nursing duties at the Kinmel Camp Military Hospital.

The Voluntary Aid Detachment (VAD) was a voluntary organisation that provided nursing services, mainly in hospitals in Britain and various other British Empire Countries and in war zones abroad. The organisation was particularly active during the First and Second World Wars. The medical services personnel they supplied included nurses, cooks, clerks, kitchen maids, ward maids, laundresses and motor vehicle drivers. During the Great War some 38,000 VADs worked in hospitals and served as other ancillary staff, they later served near the Western Front, in Mesopotamia and at Gallipoli. Vera Brittain (author of *Testament of Youth* (1933), Amelia Earhart (the aviation pioneer) and Agatha Christie were VADs.

Held in the Imperial War Museum are fascinating letters written between 21 April and 8 June 1917 by Ida Haigh during her time at Kinmel Camp to her parents in Bradford. They give an insight into Kinmel Camp at that period from a non-military angle. Ida was at Kinmel Camp until January 1918, when she was posted to Egypt.

On 21 April 1917, she began writing at 1.46 a.m.:

> Hut 16 'the spotted fever boys'. Hut 15 'consumptive patients', but all convalescent and just waiting their discharge. Hut 13 put a foment on the boil. The shops in Rhyl aren't at all bad. The road is more or less busy – Dispatch Riders on motor cycles, parties of men marching, Orderlies exercising officers' horses and many couples of military Police – there is not much chance of a poor Tommy getting out of bounds under the eagle eye of the Red Hats.

An extract from her letter of 2 May 1917:

> Another glorious warm day over. The new quarters at No.10 Camp are pretty well complete now, so the night staff has its own mess room and sitting room.

Military Swimming Gala held at Rhyl
On the Friday in the first week of June 1917, a military swimming gala was held at the Rhyl swimming baths for soldiers stationed at Kinmel Camp. A total of 382 soldiers

entered the various competitions. The Patron of the event was the Commander of Kinmel Camp and the Brigade, Brigadier-General E. B. Cuthbertson, CMG, MVO.

Visit of the Chaplain-General to Kinmel Park Camp

At the end of the first week of June 1917, the local newspapers were announcing that very soon the Chaplain-General, Bishop Taylor-Smith, would be making an official visit to Kinmel Camp and that his visit was eagerly anticipated.

The Chaplain-General duly arrived and was the guest for the weekend of the Bishop of St Asaph. On Saturday afternoon, 16 June 1917, a large number of officers from Kinmel Camp attended a garden party held in the Palace grounds for them to informally meet the Chaplain-General.

On the following morning, four separate 'immense' (according to the *Rhyl Journal*) military parade services were held at Kinmel Camp, the first one starting at 9.30 a.m. The Chaplain-General gave an address at each of the four services, all of which were held in the large Church Army Hut at Kinmel Camp. The main theme of his address(es) was 'The Dignity of Mankind'. The Chaplain-General was described as being a powerful speaker who always made a deep impression with his oratory.

A Further Concert given by an OCB from Kinmel Park Camp

The 30 June 1917 edition of the *Rhyl Journal* reported that on Sunday evening, 24 June 1917, a concert party of 17th Officer Cadet Battalion from Kinmel Camp returned to the Pavilion, Rhyl, to give a further concert for the public. It was said that their previous concert had proved quite a revelation in respect of the talented performers on display – but that this second concert 'more than fulfilled expectations, every item of a varied programme giving great satisfaction and pleasure'.

An Eisteddfod to be Held at Kinmel Park Camp

> Arrangements are well in hand for holding a Chair Eisteddfod on a large scale at Kinmel Park in September next and prizes of up to £100 are offered. The Prime Minister (the Right Honourable David Lloyd George) is expected to preside at one of the meetings.
>
> *Llais Llafur – Labour Voice*, 7 July 1917

Marriage of a Quarter-Master Sergeant from Kinmel Park Camp

It was announced in the local newspapers in mid-September 1917, that the marriage had taken place at Rhyl of Quarter-Master Sergeant Gromett from Kinmel Camp and Miss Myfanwy Davies of Minafon, Abergele. The bridesmaid was Miss May Powell and the best man was Sergeant Jones, who was also from Kinmel Camp.

A Variety Show at Kinmel Park Camp

In late September of 1917, an advertisement appeared in a number of newspapers including in the *Liverpool Echo*, for a Variety Show in aid of the 'Concerts at Front Fund', that was to appear at a number of theatres, including some in north Wales:

LENA ASHWELL VARIETY CONCERTS
(In Aid of 'Concerts at Front Fund')

GEORGE BURGESS	KATHARINE KENDALL
In Songs at the Piano	With a £2,000 Strad.

MARION KEIGHLEY SNOWDEN   GERTRUDE HIGGS
The Brilliant Pianist   The Famous Contralto

CLARA HUBBARD   BARRY LINDON
London's Finest Reciter   The Comic Basso-Profundo

TOM BURROWS   ARTHUR MELROSE
Conjurer & Ventriloquist   The Trick Whistler

MANN & BERGER, the Duettists

Rhyl Pier Pavilion, Sept. 27th at 3.
Colwyn Bay Pier Pavilion, Sept. 28th at 3.
Kinmel Park Garrison Theatre, Sept. 30th at 8.30.
Chirk Public Hall, Oct. 1st at 3 and 8.
Wellington 'The Rink', Oct. 2nd at 2.45 and 7.15.
Llangollen Town Hall, Oct. 3rd at 8 O'clock.
Shrewsbury School Speech Hall, Oct. 4th at 3 and 8.
Oswestry 'The Rink', Oct. 5th at 6.30 and 8.30.
Wrexham 'The Rink', Oct. 7th at 8.15.

**The Variety Concert will be given exactly as in France
to the Troops.**

The Garrison Theatre at Kinmel Camp came about because
of one man, who would later become world famous as a film
producer, director and the founder of ENSA. That man was
Basil Dean, who was born on 27 September 1888, at
Croydon, Surrey. In 1911, aged just twenty-three, he was
appointed as the first Director Manager of the Liverpool
Repertory Theatre (later to be called the Liverpool
Playhouse) and was also its Actor Manager.

At the outbreak of the Great War he joined the Cheshire
Regiment. But it was not fighting or anything of that nature
for which Basil Dean was destined during that war, or
indeed the subsequent Second World War: for him it was

the world of entertaining, particularly those who were in the military. In 1916 Basil Dean was stationed at Park Hall Military Camp, Oswestry, Shropshire, when he was asked to organise a Concert Party Competition to raise morale within their Battalion. The success of this venture led to the construction at Park Hall of the Garrison Institute and Theatre. Here twice-nightly performances were given, seven days a week. Later Basil Dean organised the building and initially supervised the running of a Garrison Theatre at Kinmel Camp.

In early 1917, he was posted to the War Office and took charge of the entertainment branch of the Navy and Army Canteen Board (NACB). In 1939 he founded the Entertainment National Service Association (ENSA) to lift the morale of wartime audiences.

Commendable Promptitude of an Officer

A Lieutenant Warwick Jones, who was recently wounded, is now on light duties at the Kinmel Camp. The other day about 500 marching soldiers were met by a runaway horse on the main road near the camp. Lieutenant Jones with commendable promptitude rushed to grasp the shaft of the vehicle to which the horse was attached and held on for a distance of 300 yards until he succeeded in bringing it to a standstill. He was commended for his actions by Brigadier General E.B. Cuthbertson, the Commanding Officer at Kinmel Camp.

Lieutenant Warwick Jones is the son of Mr Edward Jones, Llwyni Farm, Abergele. He has a brother, Edward Jones, studying at Cadet School in Surrey.

Abergele and Pensarn Visitor, 17 November 1917

Visitors at Easter

The *Abergele and Pensarn Visitor* reported on 6 April 1918
that there had been a very large influx of visitors to the
Abergele and Pensarn areas for the Easter Holidays, the
great majority of these visitors being the relatives of soldiers
who were in training at nearby Kinmel Camp.

New Huts especially for Women at Kinmel Park Camp

On the afternoon of Saturday 13 April 1918, two opening
ceremonies took place at Kinmel Camp. In the first
place, Mrs Cuthbertson, Wife of Brigadier-General
Cuthbertson, formally opened the new WAAC Hut and
later the Duchess of Westminster opened the new portion of
the YMCA's Camp 4 Hut and the renovated part of the old
building.

The new Hut was for the exclusive use of the members of
the WAAC and was said to have been comfortably
furnished. At the eastern end of the building a hostel for the
women had been erected. After this opening and the
inspection of it that followed, the opening of the larger
YMCA Camp 4 Hut took place. This renovated and nicely
furnished room in the main YMCA building at the camp
being for the sole use of women – namely the WAAC's and
nurses of the various nursing organisations present at
Kinmel Camp.

Intoxicants Banned for Sale to the Under-18s

Later in the war Young Soldier Training Reserve Battalions
were stationed at the Kinmel Camp. These young men
underwent military training; if the war had dragged on into
1919 and beyond, they would have been further 'cannon
fodder' to be sent to the Western Front or beyond.

Whilst at Kinmel Camp these young men, too young to
be 'lawfully' sent to the Front to fight, were amongst older

soldiers, many of whom had been on active service. These young soldiers were subject to the temptation of the 'Demon Drink' that was available at the camp. This article relates to a decision on this matter and appeared in 14 June 1918 edition of the *Cambrian News and Merionethshire Standard*:

> The North Wales Free Church Federation, at its annual meeting at Rhyl, adopted a resolution expressing pleasure and gratitude at the action of the authorities at Kinmel Park who have forbidden the sale of intoxicants to soldiers under eighteen years of age and pressed for similar steps to be taken at other camps. This is a step in the right direction which is calculated to earn for the authorities the gratitude of the parents of the boys torn by the exigences of the country from their home surroundings at an immature age. Lord Roberts was no milksop, but his views on the temptation thrown in the way of young soldiers are well known, and Lord Kitchener's soul-stirring appeal to the original expeditionary force on leaving these shores for France will long live in memory.

A Young Soldier Nearly got Shot Trying to Steal a Horse
Llais Lafur – Labour Voice of 20 July 1918 carried this piece under news from Tycroes, a village near Pantyffynnon in Camarthenshire:

TYCROES BOY'S PRANK
An eighteen-year-old lad in khaki giving the name of Evan Henry Williams, Glanewmbychan, Tycroes, Pantyffynnon, Camarthenshire, was charged at Rhyl on Saturday with stealing a horse valued at £74, the

property of a farmer near Kinmel Camp. Evidence was given that at about midnight the farmer was aroused by the disturbance of his horses and found one had been lassoed. The accused started to run away at the farmer's approach, but stopped when the farmer threatened to shoot him. He afterwards stated that his intention was to ride home on the horse to see his mother. Accused on being committed for trial, burst into tears, and said he had been at the camp eight to ten months, and was anxious to see his mother.

This young soldier was Private Evan Henry Williams, of one of the Young Soldiers' Battalions stationed at Kinmel Camp. He was born in 1900 at Llangylfelach, Glamorgan, to Jonah Williams and his wife, Martha. They were a farming family and at the time of the 'prank' were residing at Blaencwmbychan Farm (not as stated in the piece above), Tycroes, near Pantyffynon, Camarthenshire. I do think that Private Williams almost certainly could ride a horse quite well, but it stretches the imagination somewhat that he was intending to ride the horse all the way home to see his mother. Today a route planner has the road mileage between Kinmel Camp and the village of Tycroes to be in the region of 155 miles – some ride home!

At his subsequent trial the jury found Evan Williams not guilty, no doubt taking into consideration his age and his genuine desperation to go home and see his mother.

A ploughing contest took place
Llais Llafur – Labour Voice of 20 July 1918 gave the details of a rather unusual competition having taken place at Kinmel Camp:

Ystradynglais Notes

Pte. W.S. Daniels of Penygorof Farm, at present training at Kinmel Park, was successful in capturing the first prize at a ploughing match held recently at the camp. He returned home on furlough on Thursday morning.

He went Absent without Leave from Kinmel Park Camp

ABSENT WITHOUT LEAVE
At a special Police Court on Friday, before John Lewis and Llew. Davies, Esqrs., a soldier summoned for being absent without leave from Kinmel. He stated that a fit of longing for his wife and family came over him and he left camp on Sunday morning for Beddgelert. He was handed over to a military escort.

Cambrian News and Merionethshire Standard,
9 August 1918

Praise for WAACs at a Recruiting Rally

On 11 September 1918, a recruiting rally was held at Pwllheli Cinema, in order to recruit more women for Queen Mary's Army Auxiliary Corps. Mrs Lloyd George, the wife of the Prime Minister, the Right Honourable David Lloyd George, spoke in strong support of more women of Wales joining the Corps and carrying out essential war-related work, thereby greatly assisting the war effort and bringing the war to a successful conclusion for Britain and its allies. She went on to say that at the outset of the war the men of the country had underestimated the capacity of women and would not trust them to do anything of importance. However, in 1918 women were experts in manufacturing guns, shells, aeroplanes and even in the shipyards they were doing work that no one ever dreamt that women could accomplish. She assured the audience present that the WAACs were well fed and were now on shorter hours and being given more time for healthy recreation and amusement now that the enemy was being beaten!

The Bishop of St Asaph was present and also spoke in favour of more Welsh women becoming WAACs, stating his satisfaction that women joining the Corps from different parts of society was helping to eliminate class differences in the country.

General Cuthbertson then spoke of the magnificent work done by the WAACs at Kinmel Park Camp where he was presently in Command.

Others at the rally spoke in strong support of more Welsh women joining the Corps, they included Colonel John Williams who believed the training the girls underwent would improve them physically and morally. He went on to say that if the boys bled for their country why should not the girls work; discipline was good in the camps and girls in the Corps were safer in the camps than in some villages and towns.

Mrs Lloyd George – Margaret Lloyd George (nee Owen) – was born at Cricieth in 1866, a daughter of Richard Owen, a well-to-do Cricieth farmer and staunch Methodist. She married David Lloyd George in 1888 and remained his wife until her death on 20 January 1941. They had five children together and she was something of a campaigner in her own right. In 1920, Margaret Lloyd George was made a Dame (the GBE) for her raising of over £200,000 for war charities.

A Recruiting Meeting for 'the WAAC's'
On the first Saturday in October of 1918, a Recruiting Meeting was held at Blaenau Ffestiniog for the Women's Army Auxiliary Corps, now called officially the Queen

Mary's Army Auxiliary Corps. Mr J. D. Davies of The Square, Blaenau Ffestiniog, took the chair of the meeting. Addresses were delivered by Major and Mrs Cowper from Kinmel Camp, Mr W. M. Owen, Miss Williams (a National Service Organiser) and Mr Edward Lloyd Powell. It was said that several recruits had enrolled that evening.

Australian Athlete Fit and Well at Kinmel Park Camp
The Referee was a newspaper published in Sydney, Australia, which contained sporting news from a variety of sports. This was a piece in its edition of 1 January 1919:

> **Athletics**
> Writing to Mr Bob Tuck of The Botany Harriers from No. 15 Camp, Kinmel Park, Rhyl (north Wales), Cadet Geo. P.S. Parke reports himself fit and well at the time of making his letter on 20 October 1918. He is looking forward to the day when he will be in the Sydney World of Athletics once more.

George P. S. Parke was at Kinmel Camp in October 1918, undergoing officer training with one of the two Officer Cadet Training Battalions (the 16th or 17th) at the camp. He was a very decent athlete and in early 1914 he took part in Sydney in what was called in those days, 'the Running, Hop, Skip and Jump' event (today the triple jump'). He was also a sprinter and at a young age an athletics administrator and organiser in Sydney.

He sent the occasional letter in to *The Referee* during his military service overseas. In March 1916, he sent them a letter when a corporal. Then in 1917, from Belgium, dated 10 July 1917, he sent them a further letter, now as a Quarter-Master Sergeant.

He survived the War and on his return home to Sydney

he continued with his athletics. In 1919, he became the Honorary Secretary of the South Sydney Amateur Athletics Club and wrote occasional contributions to the athletics column of the *Evening News*, Sydney.

3

Accidents, Sickness and Death

Two soldiers drown at Rhyl in separate incidents
Two soldiers from Kinmel Camp drowned on Thursday, 3
June 1915, at Rhyl, in two totally separate 'incidents' and the
circumstances of their deaths were also completely
different:

> RHYL FATALITIES
> Two soldiers lose their lives by drowning.
> Two drowning fatalities occurred at Rhyl last night.
> Private T. R. Armstrong, 2nd Rhondda's of School
> Street, Wattstown, disappeared while bathing under
> the pier at low tide. His body was shortly afterwards
> recovered, but life was extinct.
>
> Two residents saw a Soldier drop into the river at
> Foryd Bridge, where there is a strong current. But all
> trace of the man was lost and dragging operations
> have proved futile up to the present. His identity is
> unknown.
>
> *Liverpool Echo*, Friday 4 June 1915

The *Evening Telegraph* covered the story on the same day
with this headline:

> SOLDIER DROWNED. ANOTHER JUMPS
> FROM BRIDGE.
> Two Tragedies within a few minutes of each other
> created great sensation at Rhyl.

On the following day, Saturday, 5 June 1915, the *Liverpool Echo* covered the inquests held into the deaths of the two soldiers:

SOLDIERS DROWNED
DISTRESSING STORIES TOLD AT RHYL
The Flintshire Coroner held an Inquest on Private Thomas Richard Armstrong, a recruit of the 2nd Rhondda Battalion, in training at Rhyl, who was drowned while bathing.

It was stated by a comrade named Private Ernest Charles Russell, that he and Armstrong and two other soldiers, none of whom could swim, went for a bathe near the pier during ebb tide. Armstrong and witness soon found themselves drawn into a kind of channel near some of the pier supports. They both went right under the water, but witness managed to get hold of a pier support and tried to help Armstrong into a position of safety, when Armstrong, however, disappeared.

The Jury returned a verdict of 'Accidentally drowned'.

The Jury also investigated the circumstances connected with the death of another 2nd Rhondda Battalion Private named Edward Akers of Gilfach, near Bargoed, south Wales.

A Rhyl Civilian named James Griffiths stated that he was walking along Foryd tollbridge, which spans the estuary of the River Clwyd, just before it enters the sea at Rhyl, when he was startled by a splash as of someone having plunged into the river, and a few yards nearer the sea he saw Akers sink.

It was stated that it was impossible for the man to fall through the bridge and Coxswain Joseph Hughes expressed the opinion that he took a header from the top of the bridge. There being no indication whatsoever that he had been fishing from the bridge, or had slipped in any way.

The Coroner said there was a great deal of mystery about the affair, and the Jury returned an 'Open Verdict'.

Private Thomas Richard Jenkin Armstrong was a son of Margaret E. Mahoney (formerly Armstrong) of 2, School Street, Wattstown, Rhondda, Glamorgan. He was born in 1898 at Pentre, Glamorgan and enlisted at Porth in 13th Battalion, the Welsh Regiment, known as 2nd Rhondda Battalion. He was just seventeen, though a number of official records have him as nineteen, which was probably due to the false age he had put on his attestation and enlistment papers. His body was returned home and he was buried at Rhondda (Trealaw) Cemetery, Glamorgan.

The soldier, who would appear to have committed suicide by jumping off the Foryd Bridge into the swirling waters below, was Private Edward Akers, who had enlisted at Bargoed. He was born in 1889 at Barry, Glamorgan, to John Thomas Akers, a Deptford-born boatman (sea) and Elizabeth Ann Akers (nee Boyce), a Somerset-born dressmaker.

The body of twenty-six year old Private Edward Akers was eventually recovered from the sea and returned home to his family. He was buried at Barry (Merthyr Dyfan) Burial Ground. Private Akers had married Elizabeth Boobyer in late 1911. Left a widow and with two young children to bring up, she married a John McElligott, the year after Edward's death,

Though the inquest returned an 'open verdict' upon the death of Edward Akers, it was almost certainly a case of suicide. He had arrived for military training at Kinmel Camp only the day before.

Two Soldiers Seriously Injured by a Motor Car

In late August 1915, shortly after 9.00 p.m. on a Saturday evening, a number of soldiers were returning on foot to Kinmel Camp from the nearby town of Abergele. At the 'S' curve at Hendrefawr, a Llandudno-owned vehicle approached towards them. Two privates of 12th Battalion the Welsh Regiment were struck by the car. Mystery was said to surround the incident in which both of the soldiers sustained severe injuries. They were firstly conveyed in the charge of an army doctor to the military hospital attached to Kinmel Camp, but were subsequently taken in a motor ambulance to the Bangor Military Hospital, to where the more serious cases were sent.

It was later ascertained that Private David Jones had sustained spinal injuries and that he had remained unconscious for more than twenty-four hours. His wife had been called to attend, so serious was his condition.

The other injured soldier, who had been dragged along by the car for several yards, had sustained head and facial injuries, with both of his legs being badly fractured. Both soldiers were said to have been due to go to the Front later that same week.

The Very Sudden Death of a Corporal

On the parade ground at Kinmel Park Camp on 15 December 1915, Corporal John Thomas Breakingbury, of 12th Battalion, the Welsh Regiment, was giving out directions for a bugle call when without any prior warning he dropped dead from natural causes. Corporal Breakingbury, born in Dorset in 1873, was forty-two at the time of his death. Prior to the War he had been living with his wife, Jane, and their four children in Gertrude Street, Abercynon, Glamorgan, where he had been employed in a local colliery as a ripper underground. He was buried at Abercynon Cemetery.

A Peculiar Fatal Accident to a Soldier

On the afternoon of Saturday 3 February 1916, Private Richard Patrick Thompson, aged thirty, of 12th Battalion, the Welsh Regiment was fatally injured in an accident. The initial account of the accident was that Private Thompson (originally of Canton, Cardiff), who had served at the Front in France including having taken part in the Charge at Loos, was on his way back to Kinmel Camp from a visit to see a dentist at Rhyl. Private Thompson and some other soldiers had hitched a ride back to camp on the buckboard of a motor lorry. But as the vehicle passed through Rhuddlan, his cap blew off. He made a grab for it and as a result fell from the moving lorry right on to his head, thereby fracturing the base of his skull on the road surface below. He died shortly after being admitted to the military hospital at Kinmel Camp, where he had been taken.

A few days later, a coroner's inquest took place. It was confirmed that Private Thompson had been wounded in France in the Charge at Loos and was convalescing at Kinmel Camp, but it had been expected that he would return to the Front in the near future.

However, an independent witness came forward at the inquest to give a different version of the events that led to Private Thompson's death. Mr Richard Sykes, the Chairman of the Rhyl Urban District Council, stated that he was driving in his car, travelling in the same direction as the lorry and came up behind it. He saw a dog coursing a rabbit in a nearby field. Next he saw Private Thompson jump off the back of the lorry as if he was going after the dog and the rabbit. When he drove right up to the now stationary lorry, he saw Private Thompson lying prone in the road. The soldier witnesses at the inquest admitted to having a dog with them, but denied that it had been coursing or in any way chasing a rabbit. A verdict of 'Death from accidental injuries to the head', was returned by the inquest jury.

Attempted Suicide by a Soldier
In the first week of March 1916, Private James Mitchell of 'B' Company, 13th (Local Reserve) Battalion, the South Wales Borderers, stationed at Kinmel Camp was charged with attempting to commit suicide. Whilst lying in his own bed in his allocated hut at Kinmel Camp, he cut his own throat with a razor. The wound was found to be only a superficial one. He was discharged to the military authorities who undertook to look after him.

Two Soldiers Killed Walking Back to Kinmel Park Camp
The Flintshire coroner, Mr Llewelyn Jones, presided over an inquest into the deaths of two soldiers from Kinmel Camp, who were killed by a motor bus in a tragic accident. Acting Corporal Robert Lewis Francis, aged forty-three, of 2nd Battalion, the Welsh Regiment, and Private Francis (Frank) Thomas, aged thirty-seven, of the same regiment, were walking back together at about 10.00 p.m. on 24 March 1916, towards Kinmel Camp, on the St Asaph Road near Nant Ddu. The inquest heard that it was a dark night and that a bus coming in the direction of the town struck the two soldiers, killing them instantly. The driver of the bus said that he did not see the two men until he was right upon them.

The coroner laid blame for the accident on the new lighting regulations, in that had the bus had upon it the usual lamps, then the two men would have seen it approach. No evidence was produced that the bus driver was travelling at an excessive speed. The accepted rule was that soldiers should walk along the roads particularly during the hours of darkness in single file, which they had not been doing on this occasion. The inquest jury returned a verdict of 'accidental death' for both of the men. They added that the county council should widen the road and that the military authorities insist that soldiers walk in single file and on the left hand side of the road at night.

Death of an 18-year-old Soldier

Robert Owen was born in 1898, at Mallwyd, Dinas Mawddwy (then in Merionethshire). He was a son of David Owen and Margaret Owen of Pandy Newydd, Dinas Mawddwy. At one time David Owen owned the Dolobran woollen mill at Dinas Mawddwy, but he died at quite a young age in 1902.

In late 1915, Robert Owen was an agricultural labourer working and residing at Cae Du, Llansannan, near Denbigh. Around this time, Lieutenant-Colonel Owen Thomas (later to become Brigadier-General Sir Owen Thomas, MP) and other prominent Welshmen were appealing for young Welsh-speaking Welshmen 'working on the land' to enlist in one of the Welsh Battalions. It is said that Robert Owen, who was just eighteen, enlisted only because a great friend of his encouraged him to enlist at the same time.

In January 1916, Private Robert Owen, 20th (Reserve) Battalion, the Royal Welch Fusiliers, was in training at Kinmel Camp. He was taken ill at the camp and was removed for a time to the camps military hospital. But as his condition worsened he was taken by motor ambulance to the Bangor Military Hospital, where he died on 1 April 1916. He was buried in the Old Cemetery, Mallwyd, Merionethshire: yet another young recruit who did not live through his basic military training let alone get to the Front and face 'the enemy' – 'Kill'em Park' was certainly living up to its name! Especially during the first few months of 1916.

Suicide of a Soldier at Kinmel Park Camp

On 10 April 1916, Private William James Jones, 13th Battalion, the South Wales Borderers, Regimental Number 33548, was found dead at Kinmel Camp. Private William James Jones, aged thirty-two, had cut his own throat using a razor, causing him to bleed to death. Death occurred quickly despite the efforts of a Royal Army Medical Corps Sergeant who was promptly on the scene, but to no avail. Private W. J. Jones was suffering from tuberculosis (TB) at the time of his death and he was a patient in the TB Ward at the Kinmel Camp Military Hospital (Camp 10). Private W. J. Jones hailed from Llyswen, near Brecon, Brecknockshire (now Powys), and had enlisted at Bridgend, south Wales. He had formerly been with the Welsh Regiment. He was buried at Abergele cemetery.

A Young Soldier's Death Discussed in the House of Commons

At the end of the first week of April 1916, some of the newspapers local to north Wales carried rather sad articles concerning the death on 5 April of Private Hughie Edwards, son of Mrs Edwards of the Lion Inn, Gwytherin, near Llanrwst. They reported that he had only 'joined the colours' a fortnight before his death of pneumonia at the Bangor Military Hospital.

But there was, in fact, far more to this story and his death was discussed in an exchange in the House of Commons on 11 May 1916. Sir H. Roberts MP questioned Mr Tennant, the Under-Secretary of State for War, about the circumstances surrounding the death of Private Hughie

Edwards of 14th Battalion, the South Wales Borderers. Hughie Edwards had originally tried to enlist in the army at Llanrwst on 9 December 1915, but had been rejected and he was handed a certificate of rejection. However, on 17 March 1916, he received an official notice calling upon him to report at Wrexham for the purposes of enlistment. Despite his earlier rejection and that he held a certificate of rejection, he obeyed the official summons and was at Wrexham passed fit for military service. Within days he was at Kinmel Camp for military training with the South Wales Borderers. Within two weeks of his being at the camp, he was, on 3 April 1916, placed most unwell in the military hospital at the camp. However, his condition worsened. On 5 April 1916 Hughie Edwards died at the Bangor Military Hospital where he had been taken the day before. He had only been on parade on one occasion prior to his death, which was attributed to his 'succumbing to pneumonia'.

Sir H. Roberts MP quizzed Mr Tennant as to why Private Hughie Edwards was passed fit for military service by the medical officer at Wrexham, having been rejected as medically unfit at Llanrwst? Also, whether he could give assurances that steps had been taken with reference to medical examinations, which would prevent the repetition of such occurrences?

In response, Mr Tennant stated that Private Edwards was called up under the Military Service Act and that he produced no evidence of ever having been rejected on medical grounds. But that he went before the medical board at Wrexham and was pronounced by them fit for general service. Mr Tennant 'claimed' that he had the facts of this case specially reviewed from a medical point of view and as a result he said there was no evidence of Private Edwards' unfitness at the time of his examination at Wrexham.

Be that as it may, Private Hughie Edwards was mistakenly sent an official 'call up' notice to go to Wrexham; the Medical Board's decision to pass him medically fit for General Army Service was a questionable one. This poor young man paid with his life for the mistakes and/or the miscalculations of the military authorities.

Private Hughie Edwards was buried at the Gwytherin (St Eleri and St James) churchyard, at a location between the church and the mortuary.

It would appear on the face of it, at least around this time, that the military authorities, when faced with medical evidence of a man being passed unfit for military service by Medical Boards at the likes of Llanrwst and Rhyl, would then engineer another such examination at the Medical Board at Wrexham. At Wrexham, that same man would be passed as fit for active/general military service: quite an indictment on the military authorities and on the Wrexham Medical Board. We can only surmise that it was a concerted plan, especially in view of the continued heavy losses of soldiers, to try to get everyone that was now being conscripted to be passed as fit for military service. Here is another example of 'sharp practice', shall we say, by the Wrexham Medical Board.

The *Liverpool Echo* of Saturday 23 September 1916 carried this story:

> FIT FOR THE MARINES
> Another complaint against a medical board was made to the Rhyl local tribunal. A motor-driver appealed for exemption and said he was first rejected by the local Doctor, but on going to Wrexham he was passed fit for active service.

Mr Edward Hughes, Solicitor, said the case was an extraordinary one. Although the man was a motor-driver, he was continuously in the hands of the doctor, yet when he went to Wrexham for medical examination before the Medical Board there, he was given a very brief examination and was told by the doctors that he was 'fit for the marines'? Not satisfied with such a decision, the man went to see the well-known specialist Dr W. Thelwall Thomas, of Rodney Street, Liverpool, who gave the man a thorough examination and certified that an operation was necessary to make him fit for service or work. In the face of such a certificate he could not see how the man could be fit for the Marines!

A local doctor who was sitting on the Tribunal said the case was well-known locally. Six months' exemption was granted to the motor-driver by the Rhyl Tribunal.

Fatal accident to a Kinmel Park Camp Soldier
At about 9.00 p.m. on Good Friday, 22 April 1916, Corporal Evan Daniels, aged fifty-three, of 'B Company', 13th Battalion, the South Wales Borderers, was walking back from Rhyl in the direction of Kinmel Camp. A car was said by eyewitnesses to be travelling towards Corporal Daniels, the car being on its wrong side of the road. The car struck Corporal Daniels and he was fatally injured, dying at the scene. The driver was subsequently told to drive with more care and should he be involved in a road traffic accident again, then it would be a serious matter for him!

Corporal Evan Daniels was at the time of his death attached to the Transport Section of 13th Battalion and was based at Kinmel Camp. His home address was in School Street, Llanbradach, Cardiff. He left a widow and a son. He was buried at Caerphilly (Penyrheol) Cemetery, Glamorgan.

Death of Private Thomas Walsh

One of the 'sudden deaths' to occur at Kinmel Camp around the time that the 'German Doctor(s) Story' was first circulating was that of Private Thomas Walsh. Private Walsh, 13th Battalion, the South Wales Borderers, died at the Bangor Military Hospital, north Wales, on Saturday, 29 April 1916. He fell ill when stationed at Kinmel Camp and was initially treated at the camp's own military hospital. But when his condition worsened, he was removed to the Bangor Military Hospital, where the more serious cases were sent to be dealt with.

The initial inquest was opened by Mr J. Pentir Williams, the coroner for north Caernarfonshire, and held at Bangor Military Hospital, Bangor, north Wales. Lieutenant Dr W. Swanson Sprent of the Royal Army Medical Corps (RAMC) based at Bangor Military Hospital, stated to the inquest that on admission to the Kinmel Park Camp Military Hospital the deceased had been violent, delirious and incoherent. When asked by the coroner if it was known at that time what was wrong with the patient, Lieutenant Dr Sprent replied:

> No, but after the patient Private Walsh had left Kinmel Park to come to the Bangor Military Hospital, as the case was deemed a most serious one, a paper was found under his pillow that contained a white powder. An emetic was then administered to him to make him vomit. The deceased Walsh had been given different remedies by other medical staff through the day, but to no effect. He was strapped down to the bed to ensure that he did not hurt himself and four Orderlies were in attendance'

When asked by the coroner if it had looked like a case of poisoning Lieutenant Dr Sprent replied:

> It might have been poisoning or mania acute. There was no smell to his breath or burning to his lips or mouth. The Post Mortem had shown the deceased to have had the body of a healthy individual and with healthy lungs. No marks or scars were found to the body of the deceased'.

Lieutenant Dr Sprent went on to say: 'At this time I cannot give a definite cause of death. But there have been cases of spotted fever at Kinmel Park Camp recently'.

The Inquest learnt that Private Walsh had been a farm labourer before enlisting and had only two months of service.

The coroner adjourned the inquest so that the stomach contents of the deceased could be analysed and for a number of witnesses from Kinmel Camp to be present to give evidence. These witnesses he regarded as important ones and stated he was 'surprised' that they had failed to attend this inquest, though they had been requested to do so.

A few days later, a second inquest was opened by the coroner for north Caernarfonshire, Mr J. Pentir Williams. An account appeared in the *Denbighshire Free Press* of this full (second) inquest reported the opinion of the medical staff, which was that Private Walsh had died from 'spotted fever' – otherwise known as cerebrospinal meningitis, of which several other cases had been reported, and two men had died of it.

The coroner alluded at the end of the inquest proceedings to the number of deaths of soldiers at Kinmel Camp, or subsequent deaths of those taken from the camp to the Bangor Military Hospital, and said that no amount of prevarication from the Senior Medical Staff at Kinmel Camp or the Bangor Military Hospital could disguise the fact that too many young men were dying at Kinmel Camp from 'disease' whilst undergoing military training.

Criticism of Conditions at Kinmel Park Camp

The 6 May 1916 edition of the *North Wales Times* reported a Bangor councillor's criticism concerning the deaths of soldiers conveyed from Kinmel Camp and its own military hospital, to the Bangor Military Hospital. Some councillors alluded to the high number of soldiers from the Bangor Military Hospital being buried at the local cemetery, but who had arrived there in the first place from Kinmel Camp and its military hospital. A quote from one councillor was that 'Too many young men are being pushed through their training too quickly in indescribable conditions at Kinmel Park Camp'.

Another asked: 'Is there a hospital in connection with the camp'? To be given the reply: 'Yes, only bad cases are sent to Bangor'.

Later in May 1916, there was a call in the press for an inspection to take place at Kinmel Camp, which was said, 'not to be in the best of condition from any point of view'. The camp was said by some observers to be 'not good enough for German prisoners, but all right from an official point of view for British Tommies'.

Death of a Hirwaun Soldier

It is with deep regret we record the death of Private Albert Matthews, late of Kendon Farm, Hirwaun. Young Matthews joined the Royal Welsh Fusiliers stationed at Kinmel Park, Rhyl. In a few weeks he was taken ill and within an hour after being taken to Hospital he died. He was buried with Full Military Honours. Private Matthews was a faithful member of St Lleurwg's Church.

Aberdare Leader, 6 May 1916

Albert Matthews was born at Merthyr, Glamorgan in 1896 and enlisted at Cefn Coed, Glamorgan, being sent for military training with 2nd Battalion, the Royal Welch Fusiliers at Kinmel Camp. His was one of the 'suspicious deaths' of soldiers that occurred during the relevant period relating to the German Doctor(s) Story at Kinmel Camp. His death at the Bangor Military Hospital was very sudden after he was taken there from the Kinmel Camp Military Hospital. He was nineteen years of age at death and was buried at Bangor (Glanadda) Cemetery, Bangor, north Wales.

A Fatal Bombing Accident at Kinmel Park Camp
On 14 June 1916, two soldiers died whilst undergoing instruction in bomb throwing at Kinmel Camp. The two men who died were Lance-Sergeant James Joseph Willoughby and Private Albert Cleaver.

Lance-Sergeant James Joseph Willoughby, 20th Battalion, the Welsh Regiment, from Pentre Ystrad, Glamorgan, was twenty-eight and married to Elizabeth Jane Willoughby. They had lived with their two children at 2, Pleasant View, Pentre Ystrad. Prior to the war he had been a coalminer hewer at a local pit, following in the footsteps of his father. Lance-Sergeant Willoughby was buried at the Rhondda (Treorchy) Cemetery.

The other soldier who died was Private Albert Cleaver, also 20th Battalion, the Welsh Regiment. He was a single man, aged thirty, of 2, Preswylfa Street, Canton, Cardiff. Private Cleaver was buried at the Marble Church, Bodelwyddan.

Four other soldiers were also seriously injured in this bomb throwing accident and were taken for treatment to the Bangor Military Hospital. The fact that the four were taken there rather than the military hospital at Kinmel Camp itself indicates that they had sustained serious injuries. The four were Captain Tomlin, Lieutenant Chatfield, Sergeant Jones and Sergeant Palmer.

At the subsequent coroner's inquest, Sergeant Franks, who was in charge of the 'bombs' for the Brigade, said that prior to the fatal bomb practice he had personally tested the grenades before issue and had found them to be in order. This fatal bomb practice involved the use of a grenade that was not thrown, but was fired from a rifle by means of a blank cartridge. But 'this grenade' that killed the two soldiers and badly injured four others did not leave the rifle. It was said that it was Captain Tomlin who was holding the rifle at the time. The inquest jury returned a verdict of 'accidental death' upon both men. The most likely cause of this 'bombing accident' was a faulty grenade that failed to 'leave the rifle' when fired – certainly not an uncommon occurrence.

The throwing of grenades/bombs at the Front was a task for the fittest and bravest of soldiers. It also entailed a decent amount of ability to be proficient at it. But this was also a particularly dangerous task even in practice, as live grenades were used. It was expected of a British Grenade/Bomb Thrower, after proper training and considerable practice, to be able to throw the grenade into a 10' by 4' trench, at a distance of some 30 yards away. Many could throw accurately even further distances. 'Throw' is a misleading term, as they were really lobbed using a bowling, cricket over-arm style, ensuring a greater height on them and a more vertical drop for them to land within a trench. A grenade that was merely 'thrown' with a low trajectory could well just hit the front of the parapet on the enemy trench. The grenades needed to drop inside the trench itself. Often a thrower could not stand up for fear of enemy fire, particularly from snipers, so they were also trained to 'bowl' and 'lob' them from kneeling and lying positions. All infantrymen received some training in 'bomb throwing' but not many became specialists at it.

The Suicide of a Brave Soldier – Lance-Sergeant Nuttall
In late June of 1916, the local newspapers were reporting that the Flintshire Coroner was dealing with a tragedy at Kinmel Camp. As on 25 June 1916, Lance-Sergeant Leonard Nuttall of 12th (Reserve) Battalion, the Royal Welch Fusiliers, had been found hanged in the Bryn Elwy Woods not far from Kinmel Camp. Lance-Sergeant Nuttall, formerly of 9th Battalion, had been wounded at the Front in France, as a result of which he had complained of loss of memory and a 'breaking up of his nerves'. The inquest was informed that Lance-Sergeant Nuttall's conduct as a soldier had been exemplary, but whilst on active service at the Front, he had been hit in the head by shrapnel.

On the ground below his hanging body, inside his cap, a letter in his own handwriting had been found and this letter was read out at the inquest by Captain Wyatt, who found the body:

> 'I Lance-Sergeant Nuttall, 13575, cannot rest day or night. My head is so bad and I deeply grieve to think of the pain and trouble it will cause. I am going to see another world. May God comfort my dear ones and have mercy upon my soul. But I am better dead than

insane and I have done my bit for England. Goodbye all. My head is bursting again now. God comfort my loved ones. Amen, Amen, Amen'

The *Rhyl Journal* of 1 July 1916 carried an account of Leonard Nuttall's death, which provides us with a few more salient details. These are extracts taken from this account:

A very sad case of suicide on the part of a soldier stationed at Kinmel Park was investigated by Mr J. Roberts Jones, deputy coroner for Flintshire, at St Asaph on Tuesday. The discovery of the tragedy was made on Sunday by Captain Wyatt, Menai Bridge, Anglesey, supervising recruiting officer for Anglesey. While on a visit to St Asaph walking through some fields near Bryn Elwy in the afternoon he noticed a soldier apparently standing under a tree. On getting a nearer view he found the soldier was suspended from the tree by a rope, his feet being about two feet from the ground. He at once cut him down, but life was quite extinct.

Information was given at the inquest by Thomas Brereton, farmer, Cefn, that stated that the deceased seemed to have been suffering from a nervous breakdown. He had not been able to sleep very well and on this account was allowed to sleep at his Mother's home in Bodelwyddan; when seen by friends last Saturday he seemed quite jolly.

Another letter was also produced at the inquest from Lance-Sergeant Leonard Nuttall to his Captain, requesting that he be allowed to revert to the rank of Private on account of his loss of memory and weak nerves due to shock. Also produced was Leonard Nuttall's Regimental Conduct Sheet that showing he had a clean record.

The inquest jury's verdict was that of 'suicide, whilst temporarily insane', which was announced by the foreman of the inquest jury, Mr John Rogers, with sympathy being expressed with the bereaved relatives for their sad loss.

Soldier from Mold found Dead at Kinmel Park Camp

On 14 July 1916, Private John Carney, aged forty-six, of 12th Battalion, the Royal Welch Fusiliers, was found dead at Kinmel Camp. The deceased had been found lying on his face, with no suspicious circumstances said to have surrounded his death. A subsequent post mortem examination revealed that his death was due to a natural cause of death, namely, 'Heart Failure'. Private Carney was born in Carrick Castle, Sligo, Ireland, and had been employed in the Mold area as a general farm labourer.

Pembrokeshire Soldier died from Illness

Arthur William Charles was born in 1897 at Llanrhian, Pembrokeshire, to Solva-born Joseph John Charles and his Mathry-born wife, Phoebe Skeel Charles (nee Lawrence). For at least a decade Joseph John Charles was a butcher and the innkeeper of the Square and Compass Inn, near Llanrhian. In 1911, they had left the inn and Joseph John Charles was a farmer at Henllys, Letterston, Pembrokeshire. The couple had a total of eleven children, six boys and five girls, with Arthur being the middle child.

Arthur Charles enlisted at Fishguard in 20th Battalion, the Welsh Regiment, known as 3rd Rhondda Reserve Battalion. He was sent to train with his Battalion at Kinmel Camp. Private Charles became ill at Kinmel Camp whilst undergoing his Initial Military Training and he was removed firstly to the camp's own military hospital; as his condition worsened he was taken to the Bangor Military Hospital, where he died on 6 August 1916, aged just nineteen. Yet another young recruit who did not live to complete his military training.

A Serious Horse-riding Accident Suffered by a General

GENERAL DUNN'S SINGULAR ACCIDENT
A singular accident befell General Dunn on Sunday 17th September 1916, as he was returning to St Asaph from Kinmel Park Camp, when his horse stumbled. The General immediately drew a tight rein in an effort to prevent the horse from falling, but the suddenness of the effort fractured his arm. He dismounted and was beginning to bandage the limb, when fortunately Colonel Cuthbertson arrived on the scene and conveyed the injured general to the camp's hospital, where his arm was attended to. He is said to be making satisfactory progress.

North Wales Chronicle, 22 September 1916

There was not to be a happy outcome to this story. Brigadier-General Robert Henry William Dunn died as a result of his serious injuries on Monday 8 January 1917, aged sixty, in a London nursing home.

Officer Mysteriously Drowned at Kinmel Park Camp
John Edmund Mathias was born at Nelson, a village some 18 miles north-north-east of Cardiff. He was born on 24 December 1878, into then a prosperous family, which later became a very wealthy family. His father, William Henry Mathias was a colliery proprietor, Justice of the Peace, and for many years a county councillor (Alderman).

John Edmund Mathias was Commissioned as a Second Lieutenant in 5th Battalion, the Welsh Regiment and he was at Kinmel Camp in the late summer of 1916, to undergo military training. He was found drowned aged thirty-seven, on Wednesday, 11 October 1916, whilst at Kinmel Camp. The Commonwealth War Graves Commission (CWGC) correctly shows the 'official' date of his death to have been Wednesday, 11 October 1916, this being the date his body was found. But other sources have it as Monday, 2 October 1916, which was the day on which he went missing and was actually last seen alive.

At the inquest at Kinmel Camp on Thursday, 12 October 1916, it was revealed that the body of Second Lieutenant Mathias had been found in an unfenced pond only some 100 yards from his hut at Kinmel Camp. A post-mortem could not reveal exactly how long his body had been in the water. A verdict of 'accidental death' was returned by the Inquest Jury, though I feel the fact he was an officer and from a wealthy, high profile family meant that 'other possibilties' as to their verdict were not fully considered. His death was indeed something of a mystery and I suggest the inquest jury should in the circumstances have returned an 'open verdict'.

Second Lieutenant John Edmund Mathias was buried in the large Mathias family grave at Llanfabon (Old) Cemetery, Nelson and he is remembered on the fine memorial to 5th Battalion, the Welsh Regiment, that stands on a hill proudly overlooking the town of Pontypridd.

Posthumous VC awarded to Soldier who underwent Officer Training at Kinmel Park Camp

Stanley Henry Parry Boughey was born on 9 April 1896 in Liverpool. He was born 'Cornes', but his mother married James Boughey, and her son took the Boughey name as his own. Stanley Boughey joined the British Red Cross Society as a serving member in wartime. By 1916 he was serving with the Ayrshire Yeomanry. From 8 December 1916 to April 1917 he underwent Officer Training at Kinmel Camp, and later found himself with his Battalion fighting the Ottoman (Turkish) Army in Palestine.

On 1 December 1917 Stanley Boughey was mortally wounded while successfully attempting to achieve the surrender of a party of thirty enemy soldiers. He was awarded the VC. Three days later he died of his wounds, aged twenty-one. He was buried at the Gaza War Cemetery.

Fatal Road Accident to a Kinmel Park Camp Soldier

Private Ernest Clark (spelt incorrectly as Clarke in some newspapers and official records), formerly with the South Wales Borderers, was in Number 2 Camp at Kinmel Camp in Christmas week of 1916. On the evening of Saturday, 23 December 1916, at about 11.00 p.m., he was walking alone along the unlit Abergele to Bodelwyddan road when he was passed by a lorry belonging to a firm of contractors who were engaged in work at Kinmel Camp. It was said that Private Clark 'fell onto the radiator of the lorry', and when picked up moments later on the roadside he was 'found to have been knocked about'. He was conveyed to nearby Kinmel Camp where, 'in spite of every attention, he succumbed to his injuries'.

The inquest was held in the first week of January 1917 by the Flintshire coroner, Mr F. Llewelyn Jones. The inquest jury returned a verdict of 'Accidentally run over'. The driver of the lorry was exonerated of all blame.

Soldiers Out Walking Seriously Injured

At about 7.00 p.m. on the evening of 26 October 1917, quite serious injuries were sustained by two soldiers from Kinmel Camp when they were out walking on the road near London House. The two soldiers, said to have been attired in 'kilties', were struck down and run over by a car. The soldiers were Privates Slater and Fiddler, both from Everton, Liverpool, and both from the King's (Liverpool) Regiment. The two soldiers had been at the camp only a few days having arrived from Park Hall Camp, Oswestry, and were on a musketry course. A Nurse Bartell from the Kinmel Camp Military Hospital initially tended to the men and an ambulance was sent for. The men, badly bruised, were subsequently taken to hospital for further treatment. I believe that both subsequently fully recovered from their injuries.

Lieutenant Found Dead in Bed at Kinmel Park Camp

Lieutenant William Reese who had been living and working in Camarthen as a bank manager with the London City and Midland Bank until enlisting, was found dead in his bed on the morning of 2 February 1917, at Kinmel Camp. He had been with 15th Battalion, the Welsh Regiment, but at the time of his sudden death he was attached to the 3rd Welsh. He had returned from service at the Front in France, suffering from concussion caused by a heavy fall from a horse and subsequently is said to have suffered a nervous breakdown. He was treated at a military hospital in London and on his recovery he was given leave to return home to his native Narberth for a short while. On 10 January he attended the Narberth Fair Day.

Lieutenant William Reese then rejoined his regiment at Kinmel Camp and had only arrived at the camp two days earlier on 31 January 1917. The day before his death he had visited the nearby town of Rhyl. The Inquest touching upon his death a few days later gave the verdict of 'Death due to Natural Causes', given the medical and other evidence presented to them.

Tragic Occurrence at Abergele

Whilst on a march from Kinmel Camp to Abergele railway station on the morning of 9 February 1917, Private William

Horatio Gay, who hailed from Stratford, London and who was with 3rd Garrison Battalion (a Labour Battalion) of the Royal Welch Fusiliers, dropped down and died on the spot. Sergeant J. H. Carmichael, who was in charge of this particular draft of soldiers, stated that the men were marching slowly near Oaklea on the Rhuddlan Road, when Private Gay was heard by Private Noel Alexander to say, 'I am done'. Private Gay then dropped to the ground dead.

Private Gay, aged forty-five, was on light duties at Kinmel Camp and was in a party of soldiers who had been marching for a total of over one and a half hours, with two rest stops on the way, when the tragedy occurred. Death was subsequently found to be due to heart failure.

Dr Peter Jones was recorded as saying, 'Private Gay was a decent man, but not quite up to soldiering'. He was buried on 17 February 1917, at the Abney Park Cemetery in the North London district of Stoke Newington. Private Gay had been a builder's labourer before the War and died leaving a wife and nine children, four boys and five girls.

Tragic Road Traffic Accident
It was on 14 February 1917, that Driver Alfred James Ellis, the Royal Army Service Corps (RASC), was killed in a tragic road accident. Driver Ellis, who hailed from Salford, Lancashire, had served at the Front in France for some time, which had resulted in a breakdown of his health. As a result, he had been a few weeks only with 490th Company at Kinmel Camp, when on 14 February 1917, he was on duty on the way to Abergele from the camp in charge of a horse and float. A Silver Motor Company bus was travelling in the opposite direction when the horse suddenly moved into the path of the oncoming vehicle and a 'head-on' collision occurred. Driver Ellis was thrown from the float and run

over by the bus, resulting in him sustaining very serious injuries. He was taken to the Kinmel Camp Military Hospital, but was pronounced dead on arrival there.

The subsequent inquest held by the Flintshire coroner Mr Fred Llewelyn Jones gave a verdict of 'accidental death', exonerating the motor bus driver of all blame.

Driver Alfred James Ellis had enlisted at Manchester on 29 July 1915 and he had fought in France. Driver Ellis' remains were reverently conveyed to Pensarn railway station by a party of soldiers from the Royal Army Service Corps, accompanied by a fife and drum. The gun carriage leading the coffin was drawn by six horses. He was buried at the Salford (Weaste) Cemetery, Salford, Lancashire.

Death of a Young Pembrokeshire Soldier through Illness

David Albert Evans was born at Cilgerran, Pembrokeshire, in 1888. When the war began, David Albert Evans was working as a gardener in Ireland and returned to Wales to enlist in the army. He attested and enlisted at Fishguard, joining 3rd (Training) Battalion, the Welsh Regiment as a Private. He was posted for military training to Kinmel Camp. Whilst at there he was taken seriously ill and died of pneumonia on 14 February 1917, in the camp's military hospital, aged twenty-eight. His body was returned home and was treated in a fitting manner. His coffin arrived at the local railway station, where it was draped in the Union Jack. A large gathering of family and friends escorted the coffin to the churchyard and he was buried in the New Ground at St Llawddog Churchyard, Cilgerran.

Camarthenshire Soldier Dies from TB

John Jones was born in 1888, in the village of New Inn, near Pencader, Camarthenshire, to Mary Jones who lived at a property there known as 'Cartref'. He attested on 9

December 1915, at Newcastle Emlyn, Camarthenshire, and was enlisted into 20th Battalion, the Welsh Regiment. He was sent for military training to his Battalion, which became a Training Reserve Battalion at Kinmel Camp, as Private Regimental Number TR4/12333. Whilst at the camp he became ill and was hospitalised for some weeks at the Kinmel Camp Military Hospital. His condition worsened and he died in the hospital on 27 February 1917, aged twenty-eight. The cause of his death was given as Tuberculosis (TB) and his body was returned to his family in Camarthenshire.

Tuberculosis (TB) is a bacterial infection that is common throughout the world. It is an infectious disease caused by various strains of mycobacteria, usually by the *Mycobacterium tuberculosis*, which normally attacks the victim's lungs, though can on occasions badly affect other parts of the body. It is an airborne infectious disease spread by an infected person to another by their coughing, sneezing or from other respiratory fluids. The cramped wooden huts at Kinmel Camp were, particularly in winter, a perfect breeding ground for the spread of such an often (especially back then) fatal infectious disease.

The Figures for Deaths at Kinmel Park Army Camp

On 7 March 1917 Mr Haydn Jones MP asked the Under-Secretary of State for War, Mr Macpherson, in the House of Commons, for the percentage of deaths amongst soldiers at Kinmel Park Army Camp, north Wales and at Park Hall Army Camp, Oswestry, for the months of October, November and December 1916; also the figures for the months of January and February of 1917. Rather surprisingly Mr Macpherson gave these figures. For Kinmel Park Army Camp they were:

October 1916:   No deaths.

November 1916: No deaths.

December 1916: 0.035%: 1 death from pneumonia, 1 from bronchitis, 2 from asthma, 1 accidental, 1 tubercle of the lung and 1 from cerebral haemorrhage.

January 1917:   0.034%: 2 deaths from asthma, 1 from pneumonia, 1 influenza, 1 syncope (brought in dead).

February 1917:   Figures not yet available.

A Shoeing Smith Dies at Kinmel Camp Military Hospital
Humphrey Davies was born on 22 October 1876, at Mochdre, near Colwyn Bay, to Thomas Davies and Margaret Davies, who both originated from Eglwysbach, Denbighshire. In 1901, Humphrey aged twenty-five, was a blacksmith residing with his parents and siblings at 128, Vale Road, Rhyl. On 29 November 1904 Humphrey Davies married Ellen Jones and in 1911, Humphrey (still a blacksmith) and Ellen were living with their three young daughters at 8, Mona Street, Rhyl.

By the summer of 1914, Humphrey was approaching thirty-eight years of age and he and Ellen had five children. Humphrey was now a shoeing smith by trade, having as a young man served a four-year apprenticeship. Humphrey was just a tad over 5' 3" in height, but was muscularly built.

In October 1914, the war was in its third month and at Wrexham on 22 October 1914, Humphrey enlisted in, of course, a Regiment or Corps that dealt primarily with horses and the care of horses. Amazingly, exactly only one week later as a 'Specially Enlisted Soldier' he was off to the Front in France to serve with the British Expeditionary Force (the

BEF) with 2nd Remount, Army Service Corps, as Shoeing Smith Davies. He was on active service in France as a shoeing smith from 29 October 1914, until 15 September 1916. During this time he is recorded as having got into trouble on one occasion, on 30 May 1915, when he was found to be 'drunk in town at 9.55 p.m.' by the military police and then to have overstayed his pass (no doubt due to the drinking!) by all of just one hour and ten minutes! For these two transgressions he received, a few days later, four days of Field Punishment No.1, as it was quaintly called by the Army (a soldier was tied to a fixed object for up to two hours a day).

Shoeing Smith Humphrey Davies became quite ill in France and on 16 September 1916 was returned to these shores and spent seventeen days as an in-patient at the Bethnal Green Military Hospital, suffering from debility following myalgia (muscle pain and often a symptom of some kind of disease or disorder, brought on sometimes by an injury or strain). With him having been a shoeing smith and all the physicality of that job, he would every working day have been under great physical strain.

On 14 October 1916, his Commanding Officer completed a 'character-type' army form on him, these being some of the things he wrote of Humphrey Davies:

> Sobriety – Very Good.
> Is he reliable – Yes.
> Is he intelligent – Fair.
> He has a Good Aptitude as a Shoeing Smith.

Humphrey was sent to convalesce at Kinmel Camp, where I am sure he would not have been idle due to his ability to work with horses. Sadly, however, his health deteriorated and he was diagnosed as having anaemia, possibly due to a viral infection he had contracted months earlier at the Front. At

5.45 a.m. on 13 March 1917, Humphrey Davies died in the Kinmel Camp Military Hospital, aged forty, of (according to the result from the post mortem) cancer of the stomach',

Humphrey Davies was buried with full military honours at the Maes Hyfryd Churchyard, Dyserth Road, Rhyl. He may not have been a frontline infantry soldier, but his abilities had been essential to the British army in France as horses played such a vital role not only as mounts for cavalry regiments, but for pulling the artillery and various other transport through the cloying mud.

His widow was granted by the Ministry of Pensions –Widows and Dependents, a pension of 31s 3d a week for herself and her five children left fatherless, whose ages were eleven, nine, six, four and two, being payable as from 17 September 1917.

A Distinct Lack of Proper Medical Care and Attention?
On 9 March 1917, it was alleged that Private Norman Humphreys of 13th Platoon, Number 2 Camp at Kinmel Camp, had, when on a drill parade, fainted and then remained unconscious for an hour. Then on 20 March 1917, Private Humphreys was ordered on parade where he was kept exposed to the cold for two hours resulting in him requiring (though not receiving) medical attention or hospital treatment. But soon after, when he saw a Dr Roberts of Corwen he was found to have a temperature of 105 and to be suffering from pneumonia.

This case of Private Humphreys was brought up in the House of Commons by Mr Haydn Jones, MP on 28 March 1917. Mr Haydn Jones also alleged that three other soldiers from Kinmel Camp also seen by Dr Roberts of Corwen had been found to have had similar high temperatures, but also had not received the proper medical attention at Kinmel Camp. Mr Haydn Jones concluded by asking what steps were being proposed by the War Office to deal with the medical officer at Kinmel Camp responsible for these cases.

Mr Macpherson, the Under-Secretary of State for War, promised that 'strict investigations would be made into these matters and that in due course Mr Haydn Jones would be informed of the result'. Sadly, I cannot find any public record of the result of Mr Macpherson's 'strict investigations'; perhaps he wrote privately to Mr Haydn Jones, though from my knowledge of such matters relating to Kinmel Camp and the War Office, I doubt whether anything whatsoever was done about this matter.

Death of Private William Luke

Private William Luke died on 13 March 1917, at Kinmel Camp. Private Luke of the Army Service Corps was at Kinmel Camp, temporarily attached to 64th Training Reserve Battalion. He was only nineteen. The inquest upon him gave the cause of death as due to 'a haemorrhage and a burst blood vessel'. It was said that shortly before his death he had appeared to be in good health and in the three weeks he had been at Kinmel Camp had only ever been away from his duties on account of being excused for vaccination and inoculation. On 10 March 1917, he had complained of a headache; later that day he fell seriously ill and became unconscious. A doctor who attended him recognised it to be a very serious case and had him quickly removed to the military hospital at Kinmel Camp. The symptoms were found to point to the brain and spinal cord and he died on the evening of 13 March. It was afterwards confirmed by a post-mortem examination that death was due to a form of meningitis. It was stated (strangely in my opinion due to previous similar cases at the camp) that no such deaths of this nature had before occurred at Kinmel Camp, but that two suspiciously similar cases had occurred around the same time. These had been under medical observation for some time and did not prove to be fatal. The inquest verdict was returned in accordance with the medical evidence.

Private Luke was buried at the Dingwall (Mitchell Hill) Cemetery, Dingwall, Ross and Cromarty, Scotland. In civilian life he had been a stationer's assistant.

A Bomb-throwing Practice Fatality
On 14 March 1917, a number of soldiers were undergoing 'Bomb Throwing Practice' in the Grenade Throwing Pit at Kinmel Camp. Live bombs/grenades were being used and four had been thrown and had exploded in the usual and correct manner. However, there was suddenly a fifth explosion that occurred close to where Second Lieutenant Arthur William Martin was standing in one of the throwing bays. In the blast, he sustained serious wounds to his head and legs.

An investigation as to what had happened took place. The only viable theory put forward was that one of the four thrown bombs had somehow set off a 'dud bomb' that had been lying buried in the Grenade Throwing Pit from a previous practice. There were strong denials by those in charge of this 'Bomb Throwing Practice' that more than four bombs were actually thrown at the time in question.

Second Lieutenant Martin, aged thirty-one, then of 61st Training Reserve Battalion, the Welsh Regiment, billeted in Camp 12, died as a result of this tragic accident, succumbing to his terrible injuries later the same day. He was buried in the nearby St Margaret's churchyard.

Death under Anaesthetic of a Sergeant
On 18 March 1917, Sergeant William Dale died whilst under anaesthetic on an operating table at the Kinmel Camp Military Hospital.

On 17 March 1917, Sergeant Dale had complained of a swelling on his neck and jaw. Seen promptly by a doctor at Kinmel Camp, he was directed to a dentist. This he did at once and on the same day he had a tooth extracted. However, on the following day he complained of feeling very unwell. He was again seen at the Kinmel Camp Military Hospital, by Doctors Smith and Robson, who found it necessary to operate upon him immediately. He was put under chloroform and died shortly afterwards, or as the report upon his death stated, 'he expired'.

The verdict of the inquest jury was 'Death from the Administration of Chloroform'. At the same time the two doctors were exonerated of all blame in the matter.

Chloroform, a colourless, dense, sweet smelling liquid was 'generally quite safe' for use as a general anaesthetic. Its strong vapours depressed the central nervous system of patients but it was known on occasions to cause cardiac failure, as appears to have been the case with regard to Sergeant William Dale.

Sickness at Military Camps – the Official View

During a Written Questions Session in the House of Commons on 30 March 1917, Mr Haydn Jones MP asked the Under-Secretary of State for War to provide him and the 'House', with the result of War Office enquiries into the state of the health of soldiers at the Litherland (Liverpool), Park Hall (Oswestry) and Kinmel Park Camps, and to the adequacy of the medical staff and of the hospital accommodation at the three named military camps.

Mr Macpherson in reply conceded that there had been an outbreak of sickness in all three camps, but pointed out that due to the recent abnormally severe weather no section of the population had escaped such sickness outbreaks. In relation to Kinmel Camp, Mr Macpherson said that the prevalent illness affecting the camp was influenza in character. He reported that the huts at Kinmel Camp were clean, well-ventilated and dry, with no overcrowding, the camp having hospital accommodation for 600 patients, with extra beds having been installed in huts. He reported that there had been thirteen deaths at the camp.

Mr Macpherson perhaps should have experienced the wooden huts at Kinmel Camp for himself, especially in winter, before spouting this utter nonsense: perhaps then quite a number of the many soldiers who subsequently died at the camp from illness and the like may have been able to leave Kinmel Camp without doing so in a coffin.

Further Figures for Deaths at Kinmel Park Army Camp

On 19 April 1917, Mr Haydn Jones MP repeated his request of some weeks earlier in the House of Commons, to be given the percentage of deaths and the causes of such deaths amongst soldiers at Kinmel Park Army Camp, north Wales, and at Park Hall Army Camp, Oswestry, this time for the latest figures for February and March of 1917.

Mr Macpherson, the Under-Secretary of State for War, gave figures for Kinmel Park Army Camp as follows:

> For February 1917: Sixteen deaths. Consisting of 1 Officer and 15 Men.
> > Pneumonia 7
> > Bronchitis 4
> > Pleurisy 2
> > Motor accident 1
> > Died at Abergele of Syncope 1
> > Found dead in quarters (an Officer) 1

> For March 1917: Eighteen deaths. Consisting of 1 Officer and 17 Men.

Pneumonia 6
Cerebro-spinal meningitis 4
Pneumococcal meningitis 1
Bronchitis 1
Meningitis 1
Dilated heart 1
Hemiplegia 1
Cancer of stomach 1
Under anaesthetic 1
Bomb wounds (an Officer) 1

Young Drummer dies at Kinmel Park Camp

The death occurred on 18 June 1917 at Kinmel Camp of John Parker Langford, a drummer with 60th Training Reserve Battalion. Liverpool-born Drummer Langford was just eighteen and was the youngest son of Thomas Parker Langford from Liverpool. His death was reported in the *Liverpool Echo*. He was buried at the Liverpool (Toxteth Park) Cemetery.

Suicide of a Staff Sergeant at Kinmel Park Camp

On 3 September 1917, Staff Sergeant Richard Ryan, formerly of the Royal Army Ordnance Corps, Service Number A.1615, then with 59th Training Reserve Battalion at Kinmel Camp was found dead. He had committed suicide by cutting his own throat from ear to ear. Staff Sergeant Ryan was a true 'Old Soldier' having previously served in the British Army during the Boer War and in India. Further investigations revealed that he served in Gallipoli where the RAOC were required for the maintenance and repair of the armaments and munitions used by the British Army.

He shared a room at the Armourer's Shop at Kinmel Camp with a Private Eggerton, who gave evidence to the inquest that Staff Sergeant Ryan had talked the day before his death of shooting himself. As a result the Private had taken ammunition from him, though that night the Private slept in another hut at Kinmel Camp. Next morning he found the lifeless body of Staff Sergeant Ryan in his hut, lying in a pool of blood, with his 'throat fearfully cut', as it was described by the Private. As Staff Sergeant Ryan had previously been on active service in the heat of Gallipoli it was pointed out that he could have suffered sunstroke whilst there, but this was not confirmed to the inquest by any medically qualified person. Under the direction of the Flintshire coroner the inquest jury returned a verdict of 'suicide whilst insane'.

Death of an Over-age Soldier from Devon

William Budd was born on about 29 January 1870, at Torrington, Devon, and not in 1872, as he told the military authorities. Budd, a builder's labourer, residing at 22, Newport Street, Stonehouse, Plymouth, Devon, voluntarily enlisted in the army on 29 July 1915, though over-age as he was forty-five. As Private William Budd, Regimental Number 32568, he was sent to Kinmel Camp to serve with 12th Battalion (Home Service), the Royal Welch Fusiliers.

William Budd became most unwell and on 20 September 1917 he was admitted to the Kinmel Camp Military Hospital suffering from bronchitis and pleurisy. His condition did not improve and on 10 October 1917 a Medical Board was convened to deal with his case. Medical reports were submitted by the Royal Army Medical Corps Doctors at Kinmel Camp Military Hospital and one stated: 'Tubercle of the Lung. Total Disablement. Kinmel Park, Denbighshire – The result of Ordinary Military Service. Exposure in training, Kinmel Park Camp 1916.17'. As a result of this Medical Board, Private William Budd was 'discharged – no longer physically fit for war service – will require Sanatorium Treatment'.

As a result, William Budd was to receive a War Disability Pension. However, on 20 December 1917, he died aged forty-seven (forty-eight on some official records) from TB whilst a patient in the Kinmel Camp Military Hospital. He was buried at the nearby Bodelwyddan churchyard.

It was Known Locally as Kill'em Park – as 'Poldark' Later Recalled!

Winston Grime (later in 1947 to change his name by deed poll to Winston Mawdsley Graham) was born at 66, Langdale Road, Victoria Park, Manchester on 30 June 1908. The Grime family had thought that eldest son, Cecil, would miss involvement in the conflict as he was not even yet sixteen when War had been declared, and surely it would not last all that long! However, it dragged on mercilessly and Cecil Grime was called up in late 1917, and was enlisted as a private in the South Wales Borderers. He was sent for his initial military training to Kinmel Camp.

In 2003, Winston Mawdsley Graham (formerly Winston Grime) the now famous author of such novels as the twelve book *Poldark* series, published his autobiography. It was entitled *Memoirs of a Private Man*. He writes of making a visit with his mother to see Cecil at Kinmel Camp:

> In late 1917, he was drafted into the South Wales Borderers and began his training at Kinmel Park, north Wales. It was known locally as Kill'em Park, because of the dozens of young men who died from pneumonia and allied diseases before they got anywhere near a German. I remember going to see him once, trailing with my Mother across what seemed like miles to a great flat camp where he appeared abruptly at the door of a wooden hut, pale and suddenly thin and with an appalling cough. Later

he was transferred to Newmarket and in the early spring of 1918 was sent to France.

Cecil Grime managed to survive Kinmel Camp and went into the firing line at the Front in France, being promoted to the rank of Acting Corporal. In around mid-1918, his Mother received a telegram from the War Office. She opened it with great trepidation, fearing that it was to notify her of the death of her son, Cecil. Shaking, she was relieved that the telegram was informing her that Cecil had been wounded, having been hit with a shell splinter on his face, just below an eye. He was exceedingly lucky, according to the Grime family, as a few inches either way would have probably resulted in the blinding, if not the death, of Cecil.

Cecil Grime survived the War and went to live in Cornwall. It was here – firstly on visits to his brother Cecil and then when living permanently in Cornwall – that Winston Graham enamoured by the area, began writing his *Poldark* novels, later to become a very popular BBC TV series.

Death of a Young Woman in the Women's Army Auxiliary Corps

Jean Roberts a young woman, voluntarily joined the Women's Army Auxiliary Corps (WAAC). She began her duties at Kinmel Camp on 28 November 1917. Jean Roberts was the main financial support for her widowed mother and five younger siblings. Sadly, Jean Roberts contracted 'spotted fever' (cerebrospinal meningitis) just weeks later, almost certainly as a result of her working at the camp. She was moved from Kinmel Camp's own military hospital to the Bangor Military Hospital, where she died of 'spotted fever' in January 1918, aged only eighteen.

Her sad death caused, some time later, on 18 November 1919, a question to be asked in the House of Commons by

Mr Haydn Jones MP. He outlined the sad details of Jean Roberts' death, adding that one of the children that she financially supported was a cripple and that no compensation was recoverable for the Roberts family under the Workmen's Compensation Act, nor under the Regulations governing Jean Roberts' enlistment in the WAAC. As a consequence, her widowed mother had been compelled to seek Poor Law Relief. Mr Haydn Jones asked whether the government, in the exceptional circumstances that he had indicated, would afford adequate financial assistance and so to remove from the poor mother the stigma of having to receive parochial relief. In reply for the government, Mr Henry Forster stated that the circumstances of the case had already been brought before the War Office and he regretted that he had no power to extend to the dependants of members of the Queen Mary's Army Auxiliary Corps who die of disease in this country, more generous treatment than that accorded to the dependants of other women employed on government work during the war. But he stated that he would consider whether it would be possible to grant exceptional treatment in this particular case.

Fire Death at Kinmel Park Camp of a Brave Officer

Now to a particularly poignant story from early February 1918. The wooden huts in the camp should fire strike them, were dangerously flammable. So it proved during the early hours of Monday, 4 February 1918. This is how this tragedy was reported in the Saturday, 9 February 1918 edition of the *Abergele and Pensarn Visitor*:

> FIRE AT KINMEL CAMP – ABERGELE FIRE BRIGADE COMPLIMENTED
> A terrible tragedy occurred early on Monday morning in No. 20 Camp, Kinmel Park. At about 3.20 a.m. the

wing occupied by officers was found to be ablaze. The alarm was raised and every effort to rouse the occupants. The wooden building burnt rapidly. Two officers and their servants managed to escape badly burned, by getting through a window. The troops fought the fire until the arrival of the Abergele Fire Brigade, under the Command of Captain Edward Williams of Moranedd. When the flames were extinguished, the whole of the wing was gutted. It was then discovered that Lieutenant Arthur Lloyd of Birkenhead, attached to a Battalion of the Manchester Regiment was missing and a search party was set to work. After a short time the officer's remains were found in a shockingly charred state and by his side the remains of a little dog, the Regimental Mascot that slept in the Officers' Quarters. Lieutenant Lloyd, an exceedingly popular officer was in Rhyl until late on Sunday night with friends, returning to Camp at about 11 o'clock.

The Inquest was held at Kinmel on the same afternoon by Mr Robert Davies, the West Denbighshire Coroner. A verdict of Accidental Death was returned. The deceased was twenty-nine years of age, single, and had seen considerable service at the Front. Lieutenant Lloyd had been the first to discover the fire, believed to have been caused by the fusing of wires. He managed to get out of the burning building, but remembering that the dog was left in the hut, went back to rescue it and was overcome it is believed. Two officers are in hospital badly burned in forcing their way out. Thanks were given to Abergele Fire Brigade for their work by Colonel A. C. Bolton. Two Lieutenants and two Privates were sleeping in the huts. Lieutenant B. Hickley was burned on the face, head and body. Lieutenant Storrs was badly burned on the face and hands.

Lieutenant Hickley and Second Lieutenant Storrs made full recoveries from their injuries; Privates Edwards and Wakefield, who had also been sleeping in the hut at the time, had narrow escapes.

Fatal Accident to an Army Service Corps Driver

On 15 March 1918, George Brooks, a driver in the Army Service Corps, was driving a horse-drawn transport vehicle from Kinmel Camp, where he was stationed, through the town of Abergele. When near to New York Terrace, Abergele, he stooped over the front part of the vehicle apparently for the purpose of taking hold of the reins. He overbalanced and fell onto the road and the back wheels passed over his thigh. Help arrived quickly and he was taken to the Kinmel Camp Military Hospital. His condition, however, worsened over a number of days and on 5 April 1918, he passed away. An inquest was held into his death, and returned a verdict of accidental death. Driver George Brooks was a native of London and a few days later his coffin was conveyed to Abergele railway station by a number of Army Service Corps men for his remains to be returned to his family for burial. He was only twenty.

A Young WAAC Dies from Illness

If you stroll through the gravestones at the Marble Church, Bodelwyddan, you will see the grave of a young woman, Doris Quane.

Doris was born at Douglas, Isle of Man, in 1898, and the family later moved to Liverpool. Doris' paternal grandfather was the impressive-sounding Caesar Bacon Quane, who worked at Holyhead Harbour, on Anglesey. He then was for many years the Chief Harbour Master at Douglas, Isle of Man. Doris' material grandfather was a Master Mariner.

Doris Quane joined the Queen' Mary's Army Auxiliary Corps as a 'Worker', as it was put. She was sent for duty to Kinmel Camp. Sadly, Doris died from an illness on 19 April 1918, and was buried in the Bodelwyddan churchyard.

A Story of Tragedy for a Neath Soldier

CAMP TRAGEDY

Neath Man who was Worried by Love Affairs

The Flintshire Coroner's enquiry into the death of Private William David Evans, a home service man, attached to a Cheshire Battalion in training at Kinmel Camp, who was cut in half by a passenger train between Rhyl and Rhuddlan, has been concluded. Evans was in civil life a tin-plate worker, residing at Tonna, Neath, and he joined the Army in January 1917.

The evidence a week ago was to the effect that he deliberately threw himself under the train and that about three months ago he tried to drown himself in a pond near Kinmel Camp. It was also stated that he was a man of peculiar temperament, regarded by some as partly insane and addicted to drinking bouts, which were followed by periods of depression.

Evans recently went away on leave in anticipation of getting married, but his love affair had apparently not gone smoothly, for the wedding did not come off. The CQMS who gave evidence a week ago admitted having misled the Jury through merely giving hearsay evidence of the attempted drowning, but he still maintained that Evans was somewhat eccentric and erratic.

A verdict of suicide was returned, the Jury holding that there was not sufficient evidence to determine the state of the man's mind.

Cambrian Daily Leader, 13 July 1918

Another Young Soldier Fails to Survive Kinmel Park Camp
Edward James Gillard was born at Bristol in 1900. He attested and enlisted in late August of 1918 and was sent for military training to Kinmel Camp in 53rd (Young Soldier) Battalion, the Welsh Regiment. Young Edward was just eighteen, only 5' 2" tall, small in frame; he became Private Gillard.

Sadly young Private Gillard, like many before him and a few after him, died at Kinmel Camp, before even completing their military training.

In late September of 1918, he was laid low with acute bronchitis and was for some nine days treated for this serious condition in the Kinmel Camp Military Hospital. But sadly on 7 October 1918, he succumbed to the condition and died. His father had received notification a few days earlier of his son's deterioration and he was able to travel up to north Wales and be present at the death of his young son, which may have been of some comfort to him. Edward's condition was said by the military authorities to have been brought on 'from the strain of his exposure to military training'. The truth was far less palatable for the military authorities to own up to: that previously fit and healthy young men were dying needlessly, due to being housed in cold, damp, cramped and totally unsatisfactory disease-spreading conditions at the wooden-hutted camp.

Private Gillard was buried at Barry (Merthyr Dyfan) Burial Ground, just four weeks from the end of the First World War, never having fired a shot in anger.

Posthumous Award of VC for Former Sergeant-Instructor at Kinmel Park Camp

Frank Lester was born on 18 February 1896 in Liverpool. By the time of the 1911 census he was an apprentice joiner. In March 1916 he enlisted in the army at Birkenhead. He was posted to 10th Battalion, the South Lancashire Regiment. Despite his age he showed a good aptitude for leadership and was soon promoted to Sergeant-Instructor for new recruits, firstly at Prees Heath Camp, Shropshire, and then at Kinmel Camp.

After some months training recruits at Kinmel Camp he was transferred initially to 2/7th Battalion, the Lancashire Fusiliers. Then to enable him to serve at the Front in France and Flanders, he had to relinquish his rank of Corporal and Sergeant-Instructor and return to the rank of Private. In December 1917, in France, he was wounded and hospitalised. In July 1918 as part of his convalescence he was sent to Cromer on the north Norfolk coast.

He returned to the Front in France in September 1918. On 12 October his Battalion became heavily involved in action with the Germans at Neuvilly, near Le Cateau. Acting courageously under heavy fire Frank Lester lost his life to a sniper's bullet whilst protecting several other soldiers. He was posthumously awarded the VC 'for most conspicuous gallantry'.

The Death of a Young Soldier from St Helens, Lancashire

Thomas Dearden was called up for military service on 28 September 1918, then attested and enlisted two days later. On 4 October 1918, he joined 53rd (Young Soldier's) Training Reserve Battalion of the Cheshire Regiment at Kinmel Camp. As Private T/R 55618, Thomas Dearden, 5' 4" tall, an electrician's labourer from Friar Street, St Helens, Lancashire, began his military training which was so very soon to cost him his young life. Within a few short days of being at Kinmel Camp he went down with an influenza-type illness of a serious nature.

At 8.15 p.m. on 14 October 1918, in the military hospital at Kinmel Camp, Private Thomas Dearden died at the age of just eighteen. The medical report on his death gave the following: 'Death due to influenza, pneumonia, gangrenous appendicitis and cardiac failure – He had an operation but failed to rally'.

British Columbia Soldier dies in Kinmel Park Camp

William Fraser McCaskill was born at Tynehead, City of Surrey, British Columbia, Canada, in 1894. During the First World War he enlisted in Canada in 1st Reserve Battalion, Western Ontario Regiment of the Canadian Infantry, as a Private. In late October 1918, he found himself at Kinmel Camp and sadly on 24 October 1918 he succumbed to illness and died in the Kinmel Camp Military Hospital, aged twenty-four. His parents were Mr and Mrs R. McCaskill of Cloverdale, City of Surrey, British Columbia.

William Fraser McCaskill was buried in the nearby Bodelwyddan churchyard, one of the many Canadian soldiers who succumbed to illness, particularly to the Spanish Flu influenza pandemic, whilst at Kinmel Camp from October 1918 and into 1919.

4

Misdemeanours

A Missing Corporal – Foul Play Strongly Suspected!
Corporal Evan Samuel Phillips of a Welsh Battalion
stationed at Kinmel Camp, went missing on 31 July 1915.
After some days had elapsed, the military and civilian
authorities strongly suspected that Corporal Philipps was
the victim of foul play. Speculation was rife when not only
the camp was searched from top to bottom, but some
unlikely places in and around Kinmel Camp were dug up in
the search for him!

However, by mid September 1915, Corporal Phillips, a
native of Glamorganshire who had formerly served with the
Metropolitan Police Force, revealed himself to be alive and
well. He had sent a communication, which the London police
had obtained, to the effect that he had arrived in New York on
15 August, and 'did not intend to return to England, although
out of work'. The handwriting in the letter was identified as
Corporal Phillips' by his brother. The Corporal wrote in this
letter of his regret at what he had done – presumably to
avoid being sent to the Front with a draft from his battalion.

However, in late November or early December 1915,
Corporal Phillips returned to Wales, was recognised by the
police, and arrested as a deserter. He was promptly handed
over to the military authorities to be dealt with – which
meant, for certain, a spell in a military prison.

A Dishonest Soldier from Kinmel Park Camp
This account of proceedings at a Court in Manchester
appeared in the Friday 12 November 1915 edition of the
Manchester Evening News:

A Dishonest Soldier
At the Manchester City Police Court, to-day, W. Beer, a private in the South Wales Borderers, in training at Kinmel Camp, near Rhyl, was charged with stealing a diamond ring, value £9, the property of Mrs Eleanor English, of Church Lane, Harpurhey.

It was stated that whilst in Colwyn Bay, Mrs English's sister-in-law made the acquaintance of the prisoner. He went with the young lady to Mrs English's house as her fiancée, and while there took the ring from a dressing table in the bedroom.

The prisoner admitted taking the ring, but said it was done on the impulse of the moment. There were previous convictions against Beer for theft and he was sent to gaol for six months.

Disgraceful Scenes on the Streets of Abergele
On the evening of Saturday, 15 November 1915, disgraceful scenes were witnessed by local persons on the streets of Abergele. A squad of soldiers from the nearby Kinmel Camp were said to have badly maltreated several employees of one of the local garages. The local council as a result were writing to the Officer Commanding at Kinmel Camp, requesting that he send more military police to the town, especially on Saturday nights.

At a special court hearing a few days later Private Henry Noble of 15th Battalion, the Royal Welch Fusiliers, was accused of the offence of 'assault on police'. It arose from the incident on Saturday, 15 November, when abusive words and actions by the soldiers took place at Mr Pierce's Abergele Garage. Private Noble, who was said to have been drinking at the Harp Hotel, Abergele, prior to the incident, was at first given the sentence of fourteen days in prison with hard labour. The prosecuting police sergeant then, however, gave some evidence to the court in favour of Private Noble, in that Noble was not the instigator of the trouble, but that other soldiers from Kinmel Camp were. Noble was spared the prison sentence and instead was fined twenty shillings and received an admonishment.

As a result of this incident the military authorities began to permanently quarter their men in the town of Abergele, much to the relief of the local council and many of the inhabitants of Abergele!

Robbing the War Office
In the third week of November 1915, the Rhyl Magistrates had appear before them two civilian labourers from Kinmel Camp. They were Patrick Kelly and Richard Jones, accused of having been in unlawful possession of bread and groceries stolen from Kinmel Camp and therefore the property of the War Office. The two accused had been found 'in the lines' at the camp with bundles of food and had made several different excuses as to how they came by the items. The two were found guilty and fined £2 each. The magistrates said that there was too much of this sort of thing going on and that they would put a stop to it.

Court Martial held – for Captain Douglas How
In the first week of January 1916, a court martial was held at Kinmel Camp with Colonel T. A.Wynne-Edwards of 21st Battalion, the Royal Welch Fusiliers presiding, that related to an incident that had taken place at Kinmel Camp on 12 December 1915. The circumstances were that Captain Douglas How from 20th Welsh Regiment was accused of having been drunk and incapable of discharging his duties as the 'Captain for the Day'. This charge was brought by Major Broad, who gave evidence to the effect that he had found Captain How in an intoxicated state when he was on duty as

the 'Captain for the Day' and as a result had ordered him to go to his room. The accused Captain How told the court martial that on the day in question he had been perfectly sober, having had but three whiskies and sodas all day! He went on to accuse Major Broad of having been in a violent temper on the day in question for some unknown reason and for blustering around the camp.

In summing up the case, court martial member Colonel Ivor Bowen commented upon the conflict of evidence presented, including the differing opinions of two military surgeons who had given evidence to the court martial, making it a difficult case upon which to reach a correct verdict. Captain Douglas How was found Not Guilty, having been represented by Mr Dew (Solicitor) of Bangor.

Captain Douglas How was to appear in the local newspapers in happier circumstances in late May of 1916. This is a story carried in late May 1916 by the *Rhyl Record and Advertiser*:

> Marriage of Captain Douglas How of 20th Welsh Regiment, Kinmel Park and Miss Amy Joy of Church Street, Rhyl. The Bridegroom left his ranch at Calgary, Canada at the outbreak of war and joined the forces. He was formerly in the 3rd Welsh Regiment and served throughout the South African Campaign with his present Colonel, Col. Sir William Watts. The couple to honeymoon at Blackpool.

Another Court Martial held – for Captain J. L. Down

A second court martial took place on the same day at the Kinmel Camp. This was for a charge of drunkenness brought against Captain J. L. Down of 21st Reserve Battalion, the Welsh Regiment, presently stationed at the camp. Captain Down had been formerly the Adjutant of

10th (1st Rhondda) Battalion, who had trained at the camp but who were now at the Front. The finding of the court martial was to be submitted to the higher authorities 'before a decision was promulgated' and for the time being the accused Captain J. L. Down was to remain under arrest.

Some weeks later it was promulgated by the military authorities that Captain J. Leslie Down, as a result of his recent court martial, had been 'dismissed forthwith from the army'.

Arrest at Rhuddlan of a 'Soldier at his Place of Work'

An unusual story of a soldier's 'apparent' attempt to evade doing his military service as required, came to light in the last week of February 1916. Private Evan Price, a native of Tonypandy, south Wales, went absent without leave from 21st Battalion, the Welsh Regiment, stationed at Kinmel Camp. He was traced to a Rhuddlan (near Rhyl) Foundry, where he was found to be working as an employee! However, he was proved to be an epileptic and as a result was discharged from military service permanently. Private Price, when interviewed, stated that he had no reason to return to his home in south Wales as 'his wife was carrying on'.

The First Boy Racers?

Local newspaper reported that in late March of 1916, there had been complaints locally relating to speeding vehicles:

> Complaints of scorching on the Rhyl Road: The police yesterday prosecuted motor drivers from the Kinmel Camp for driving to the danger of the public. Particularly after the soldiers had received their pay. There was a stream of cars racing between the camp and Rhyl. Accidents were happening and a number of

people were now in hospital as a result. Taxis were driving towards Rhuddlan at busy times at 25 to 30 miles per hour, without sounding their horns. Buses must keep to 12 miles per hour. Colonel Howard the Chairman of the Magistrates, deplored the situation.

YMCA Worker Committed for Trial

The story broke in the press in early April 1916, that a Henry Matthews, also known as Percy H. Clark and by a string of other names, had been residing at Morfa Lodge Farm, Rhuddlan, near Rhyl, for some weeks. This man had been brought before local magistrates on charges of obtaining a banker's cheque and order for payment of twenty-one shillings from a Mr Austin Pywell and for obtaining fifteen shillings by false pretences from a Mr Thomas Gretton. 'Henry Matthews' had also been going under the name of A. Harrison when pretending to be a government official engaged in surveying the land for taxation purposes, falsely obtaining various sums of money from several local farmers. 'Matthews' was said to have lived an adventurous life and was described to the court as a very clever and plausible man. This crooked confidence trickster was committed to the Staffordshire Assizes where he faced a number of other similar criminal charges and a warrant for his arrest issued in Staffordshire, was already in existence. 'Matthews' was said to be able to speak both German and French.

In late June of 1916, Henry Matthews, which was 'believed to be' his real name, appeared before the Wednesbury, South Staffordshire, Magistrates' Court. Mr J. J. Sharpe, for the Director of Public Prosecutions, outlined the many charges against Matthews and alluded to him being something of a Jekyll and Hyde character. Prior to committing the offences in north Wales, Matthews had been fraudulently extracting monies from various farmers in the Great Barr District when falsely claiming that he was either an official of the Board of Agriculture or from the Ordnance Survey Department.

Mr J. J. Sharpe informed the court what was known about the prisoner Matthews: that his boyhood was spent in the locality of West Bromwich, that he became an expert draughtsman and surveyor, later working in offices at Liverpool and in the offices of the Manchester Ship Canal. In 1907, Matthews met Father Ignatius of Llanthony Abbey, studied under him and subsequently visited the Westphalia and Alsace regions. Then he entered a monastery, took the vows of a Roman Catholic Priest, went to Rome where he obtained an interview with the Pope and received a dispensation from His Holiness! Returning to England, Matthews was next heard of doing missionary work under the Bishop of Rochester. In 1914, he was in the Great Barr District and later visited Rhyl, where he did much work in the YMCA at Kinmel Camp. This work included preaching to the soldiers at Kinmel Camp whilst living in the house of a curate. Whilst driving the latter's motor car around the district, he found himself in the hands of the military when seen taking photographs and making plans in the vicinity of the camp.

After investigations by the military at Kinmel Camp, it had been decided that Matthews was not a spy, but a conman who used the photographs and plans as props to fool those he was trying to obtain money from. He would get the farmers to pay him for the photographs and plans purporting that these would help them pay less tax on the land they owned. It was lucky for him that the military concluded this or he would have been facing a firing squad! Matthews was proved by an official of the Survey Department not to be a bona-fide official of theirs and was remanded in custody, being committed for trial at the Staffordshire Assizes.

A Motoring Offence

In the first week of April 1916, Lieutenant John George Prosser, stationed at Kinmel Camp, was fined £5 at the local magistrates' court, for the offence of riding a motorcycle through Rhuddlan (near Rhyl) with an acetylene lamp burning brightly. The court was informed that he had been warned on three prior occasions for doing this, but was said to have acted in a grossly impertinent manner when spoken to about the matter. The chairman of the magistrates, Colonel Howard, said during the hearing 'that officers should learn habits of discipline and that they had to obey the law like everyone else'.

Liquor Offence at Rhyl

Under New Liquor Control Order
Case Heard at Rhyl Petty Sessions
The licensee of the Mostyn Hotel, High Street, was charged with contravening the above order by supplying through his servant, Annie Archer, stout to Sergeants John Henry Morris and Albert Marsh of 21st Battalion, the Royal Welch Fusiliers, stationed at Kinmel Park Camp, during prohibited hours on Sunday, 15th March. Sergeants to pay costs.

Rhyl Journal, 15 April 1916

The Mostyn Hotel, Rhyl, stood on the corner of High Street and Wellington Road. The licensee and proprietor charged above was Mr A. W. James, who for many years had previously been the proprietor of the Grosvenor Temperance Hotel, Rhyl.

Two Soldier Thieves Jailed

In the first week of May 1916, two soldiers from Kinmel Camp appeared at the Rhyl Magistrates Court charged with theft. The two privates, Richard Hyslop from Oldham, Lancashire and Thomas Yowatt from Neath, south Wales, were accused of the theft of a purse containing a railway ticket and two shillings in cash, the property of Margaret A. Roberts of Brook House, Rhuddlan, near Rhyl. Both men were found guilty, with each of them being sentenced to one month's imprisonment with hard labour.

Private Richard Hyslop would appear to have been something of a serial offender when it came to thieving, though he was not very adept at avoiding being caught. However, this could have been a rather clever ruse by him to commit a crime and be jailed for the offence, thereby escaping being sent out with a draft from Kinmel Camp to the Front in France or elsewhere. He would not have been the first or indeed the last to use this drastic, but effective method of remaining in this Country, 'safe' in one of His Majesty's Prisons!

Serious Charges of a Sexual Nature made against a Lance-Sergeant

Lance-Sergeant George William Hermitage of 'B Company', 13th Battalion, the South Wales Borderers, was on sick leave at Kinmel Camp in April and May of 1916. On Friday, 12 May 1916, he appeared before the Rhyl Magistrates on one charge of indecent assault and two of indecent behaviour, or as a local newspaper put it, 'of molesting women'.

The court heard that Lance-Sergeant Hermitage was accused of indecent behaviour towards a Mrs Pasquille, of 'manhandling' the eight-year old daughter of Mr George Rust and of having indecently exposed himself to two ladies in the vicinity of Kinmel Camp. These two ladies were the wife and daughter of Sergeant Major Cotterill, of the Shropshire Light Infantry. An identification parade was then held with nineteen other sergeants from Kinmel Camp being 'mustered', as it was put, to go into the line-up with Lance-Sergeant Hermitage. Hermitage was picked out as the offender at the identification parade by one of the adult female witnesses.

Lance-Sergeant Hermitage denied the charges, claiming that with regard to the latter alleged offence he was in fact some two miles away from the said location at the time. In his own defence to the court, Hermitage stated that he had fought in China with the British Army and when war broke out, he re-enlisted. He was however at the present time on home sick leave. An officer from his company gave evidence that Hermitage was of excellent character and that he had shown personal bravery on the field of battle in France. He was, however, found guilty of all three alleged offences and was sentenced to two months' imprisonment with hard labour for each of the three offences, making a total sentence of six months with hard labour.

A Civilian Assaulted by a Soldier

In the first week of June 1916, Mr Thomas J. Jones, a Rhyl Builder, residing at 18, Kinmel Street, Rhyl, gave evidence in the local Magistrate's Court against a soldier. Mr Jones alleged that on the evening of Sunday, 23 May 1916, he was walking along the Rhyl Promenade when the defendant Private W. Owen of the Welsh Regiment, stationed at Kinmel Camp stopped him and asked him for money for drink. When he refused, the defendant Private Owen became abusive and struck him with great force in his eye, using a fist, causing Mr Jones to be rendered half-conscious. When replying to the charge, the defendant Private Owen said that he had already been punished for this offence of assault by the military authorities at Kinmel Camp.

Private Owen was fined ten shillings by the court, with the remarks by the magistrates that it was unpleasant to have one of His Majesty's soldiers appear before them.

Battalion Postman Steals

In the third week of July 1916, Corporal William Morgan Gould, a Battalion postman stationed at Kinmel Camp, was found guilty in court of stealing letters and parcels at the camp. Two test parcels had been prepared and Corporal Gould was caught out stealing them. He was sentenced to three months imprisonment with hard labour for each offence, therefore to a total of six months imprisonment with hard labour.

Stole a Pony

In the fourth week of July 1916, two drivers in the Army Service Corps, stationed at Kinmel Camp, Henry Jones and Gilbert Trigg, appeared in court on a charge of having stolen a pony valued at £21 from Mr Robert Roberts of Bryn Tywydd, Abergele. The stolen pony was traced to Fron Wen, Llansannan, where the two drivers had sold it to the occupant for ten guineas.

Soldier Absent without Leave from Kinmel Park Camp

This small piece appeared in the *Cambrian News and Merionethshire Standard*, 4 August 1916:

Aberayron News

Police Court – On Monday, John Thomas of Sarnau, Llanarth, was charged by P.C. Oliver with being absent without leave from the 21st Battalion, Welsh Regiment, from Kinmel Park. On the 26 July he was remanded to wait an escort.

A Sergeant Caught Poaching – Allegedly!

In the first week of August 1916, Sergeant J. Pedlar, stationed at Kinmel Camp was charged with the offence of poaching. He was caught snaring rabbits on the land of Colonel H. B. L. Hughes. In answer in court to the charge, Sergeant Pedlar, who was in a Non-Combatant Corps, claimed that a tenant whom he believed had grazing rights over the land had said that he could catch rabbits on it.

A Sergeant Deserter from Kinmel Park Camp

Sergeant Joseph Parry from one of the Royal Welch Fusilier Battalions stationed at Kinmel Camp and a native of Rhyl, donned civilian clothing and tried to hide his khaki uniform on the Rhyl Golf Links. But his uniform was found by the military. Having roamed about the golf links for some time, he got tired and bored, which resulted in him giving himself up. In late August of 1916 he was on remand and awaiting a military escort, a court martial, and probable time to serve in a military prison.

A Deserter is Caught by Good Detective Work

In the second week of October 1916, Police Constable Henry Jones was present on the platform at Rhyl railway station when he became suspicious of a man who alighted from the 8.25 train. The man looked dirty and unkempt and was not wearing puttees, though he appeared to be a soldier of some kind. Believing the man to be a deserter, PC Jones arrested him. Subsequently this man, Private John Sullivan of 3rd Battalion, the Welsh Regiment, was charged with being Absent Without Leave from Kinmel Camp. Private Sullivan was in the process of deserting and returning to his home address in Cardiff, from where he had only just arrived at the camp. He was remanded in custody to await a military escort.

The Magistrates awarded PC Jones the sum of five shillings (25 pence in today's money) for his diligent work and told him that they believed that he would make a good detective.

Puttees are today one of the most recognisable features of a British Soldier from the Great War. Indeed they were also worn by other Armies including the Australian Army and the United States Infantry. They were woollen leg wrappings, often some nine feet in length, with cotton tapes on the end to tie them off with. Being worn in order to stop water and mud from getting into the boots and issue trousers of soldiers. They also provided support to the legs, but were not the easiest things for a soldier to put on quickly and correctly. Puttees were dyed to match the required colour of the soldier's uniform. The word 'puttee' being derived from the Hindi word 'pattah', meaning a strip of cloth.

Embezzlement at Kinmel Park Camp
On 23 December 1916 John Lyttleton, a barman from Rhyl, pleaded guilty in court to the charge of embezzlement at one of the canteens at Kinmel Camp, amounting to £4 8s 11d. He had been traced and apprehended in his married sister's house in Liskeard, Cornwall, where he had fled. The defendant a civilian appeared in court wearing Boer War active service colours. If he thought that this 'ploy' could keep him out of prison then he was much mistaken. The court heard that on a previous occasion he had served two months' imprisonment with hard labour for a theft offence in London. For this offence he was sentenced to three months' imprisonment with hard labour.

Two Soldiers Committed to the Assizes
At the Rhyl Police Court on Friday, 5 January 1917, appeared two soldiers from Kinmel Camp on two separate

shop-breaking charges, namely Privates Reginald James Birchroyd and George Williams, both of 3rd Battalion, the Welsh Regiment.

In the first case, Mr George Parry, a Rhyl grocer, stated that his lock-up shop at 35, Wellington Road, Rhyl was securely locked up at 8.00 p.m. on 20 December (1916). At 7 a.m. the next day he discovered that the premises had been forcibly entered, with two doors having been forced open, some bricks removed and a bolt broken. He found to be missing a cheque book that contained twenty-three unused cheques, a tin of lobster, three tins of fruit, three loaves of bread and three shillings in copper coins: a total value missing of nine shillings plus the cheque book.

Police Sergeant Owen Jones then gave evidence that with the assistance of Police Constable Charles Millington he arrested the two soldiers Birchroyd and Williams in Ffynongroew Road on 26 December (1916). On searching them he found the stolen cheque book belonging to Mr George Parry in the possession of Birchroyd. In reply to the charge Williams said, 'I know nothing about it. This is the first I have heard of it'. However, Birchroyd said in reply, 'We will own up to it'. To which Williams then changed his tune completely and said, 'I will own up too'.

In the second case against them, Mr Domenico Sidoli, a Rhyl confectioner, stated that he had a lock-up shop at 32, Wellington Road, Rhyl, which was closed during the winter months. He stated that he had left the premises quite secure after his last occasional visit there on 22 December (1916). However, on 24 December another witness in this case had visited him to inform him that he had better go to check on his premises. He did so and found that they had been broken into. A window and a door had been forced open and another door had then been unlocked. A portmanteau and goods to the total value of two guineas were missing.

Police Sergeant Owen Jones was then able to enlighten the court by informing them that the portmanteau and other items belonging to Mr Domenico Sidoli, including one of his business' trademark hats, had been found in a stockyard off Marsh Road, Rhyl. When questioned about this shop-breaking, Private Birchroyd replied, 'We were both together when we did it'. Private Williams was less forthcoming and when questioned replied, 'I will say nothing'.

The magistrate's clerk stated that several charges were pending against the two soldier prisoners and thanked Superintendent Lindsay for his valuable help with the depositions. The two soldiers were to remain in police custody and were committed to the assizes.

Mr Domenico Sidoli was an Italian immigrant who from 1910 at 32, Wellington Road, Rhyl, ran Sidoli's Café and Ice Cream Parlour. The business is still in existence today in Wellington Road, Rhyl and continues to be run by members of the same family.

Blinded by the Light!

The *Rhyl Journal* of 6 January 1917, gave an account of a serious road traffic accident that had taken place a few nights earlier. A Mr John Williams, a bailiff at Pengwern Home Farm had been knocked down on the Rhuddlan railway bridge by a soldier from Kinmel Camp who was riding a motor cycle. Mr Williams was badly cut about the head and after being attended to by Doctor Henry Lloyd of St Asaph, he was conveyed for further treatment to the Denbigh Infirmary.

Mr Williams attributed the accident to the blinding light of the motor cycle that hit him as he was walking over the bridge.

Scene Caused at Llanrwst by Soldiers Looking for 'Skulkers'

On the Friday evening in the first week of January 1917, 'three men in khaki' visited several hostelries in the town of Llanrwst, claiming to be searching the town for 'skulkers'. They proceeded to stop every man of military age that they came across and ordered them to produce their Exemption From Active Service Cards, under the threat of immediate arrest if they failed to do so. The result it was said was that 'a spirit of unrest and insecurity permeated through the under-41 year old members of the community'.

However, the local police, suspecting the motives and indeed the jurisdiction of the 'three men in khaki', called upon them to produce their passes. It soon transpired that the 'three men in khaki' were actually themselves deserters from Kinmel Camp.

On the following morning (Saturday) the three deserters appeared in a special court before Mr O. Isgoed Jones and were remanded in custody to await an army escort on the charge of being deserters from 4th Battalion, the Welsh Regiment, stationed at Kinmel Camp.

Did Not Want to Fight, so got Himself Arrested by the Police – Again!

The *Rhyl Journal* of 13 January 1917 carried this short piece:

Did Not Want To Fight

Police Constable Millington of Rhyl found Private Richard Hyslop of 7th Battalion, the South Wales Borderers in a shed at the back of the premises of Mr Jno. Williams, the photographer, of 23, High Street, Rhyl. He was hiding there to avoid being sent out to France with a draft from his Battalion. Magistrates handed him over to the military so that he could do his duty as a soldier.

Captain Blowen of Kinmel Camp made the following statement in court with regard to Private Richard Hyslop: 'The man has a bad record and was convicted at St Asaph for stealing a purse, for which offence he went to prison for one month'. It was Captain Blowen who had appealed to the court for them not this time to imprison Hyslop, as that was what he probably wanted in order to escape overseas service at the Front, but instead hand him over to the military authorities and he would be off to the Front in the very next draft from his battalion. This was acceded to. Hyslop had been caught at the rear of Mr Jno Williams' photography studio premises gathering together cardboard boxes with a view to starting a fire. The charge laid against Hyslop in court had been, 'being found on enclosed premises'.

A Case of Bigamy
In March of 1917, Army Sergeant John Solari, aged thirty-five, of 62nd Training Battalion, based in Camp Number 1 at Kinmel Camp, appeared in court accused of bigamy. The Court heard that Sergeant Solari had on 18 November 1916, at St Asaph District, married Hannah Davies of 1, Railway Terrace, Prestatyn. The problem was that he had on 6 April 1907, at St Mary's Roman Catholic Church, Wrexham, married one Johanna Prendegast, from whom Solari was not divorced and who was very much alive and therefore still his 'lawful wedded wife'. The second marriage to Hannah Davies was therefore bigamous.

John Solari pleaded guilty and said that his first wife neglected their children and that he was unhappy with her. Superintendent A. E. Lindsay informed the court that the prisoners 'legitimate' wife had indeed been before the courts on a charge of neglecting her (and the prisoner John Solari's) children.

The court heard that Solari had an excellent fifteen-year record of army service, but that did not stop him receiving a prison sentence of three months for the offence. During the case the magistrates warned women to be wary of such liaisons with soldiers at Kinmel Camp.

Another Case of Bigamy

Around the same time as the above case, another bigamy case had reached court involving a soldier from Kinmel Camp, which was also reported upon in the local newspapers. A Private Joseph Jones, formerly of 16th Lancers, aged thirty, was said to have on 5 April 1916 at St Asaph, under the false name of Thomas Gray, 'feloniously' married one Hannah Jane Hughes. It was alleged in this special court that Private Jones had told Hannah Hughes, a domestic servant of 28, Wellington Road, Rhyl, that he was a bachelor, which was untrue. Before enlisting in the army, Private Jones was said to have worked on farms in the Mold and Wrexham areas. In his own defence, Private Jones claimed that Hannah Hughes had known his real name all along and that it was in fact her idea for him to change his name and enlist at Kinmel Camp, he having formerly been at the Prees Heath Camp.

He went on to say that Hannah Hughes was living with her 'cousin' from Liverpool when she persuaded him to marry her, threatening to do away with herself unless he did so. The court, having been presented with the proof that Private Joseph Jones' first and legitimate wife was alive and well and living in Bwlchgwyn, near Wrexham, did not appear to believe his version of events, as he was subsequently found guilty and sentenced by the court to three months' imprisonment.

Kinmel Camp Theft Charge

In mid-June of 1917, Private Evan Davis, described in court as a Battalion Butcher of the 58th Training Reserve, stationed at Kinmel Camp, was found guilty of stealing and then selling on fifteen and a half pounds in weight of beef, belonging to the camp. He was fined and bound over for twelve months.

A Bicycle Thief

In July of 1917, Private Thomas Williams of Number 5 Camp, at Kinmel Camp, pleaded guilty in Court to stealing a bicycle valued at £2 10s., the property of Mr Rose of Rhuddlan. Mr Rose had left his bicycle unattended at the sewage works at Kinmel and when he returned to the location a short time later, it had disappeared.

The bicycle was subsequently found in Private Williams' home city of Liverpool. Private Williams was sent to prison for three months with hard labour and the magistrates stated that 'it is hoped that when he comes out of prison he will be met by an escort and taken to serve in France'.

Two Young Soldiers Accused of Stealing

Two young soldiers from Kinmel Camp appeared before Mr B. Wadsworth, Magistrate in the Rhyl Police Court at the beginning of the second week of August 1917. The two, said to be youthful-looking, were John Hepton and Frederick Gordon Young who stood accused of two theft offences committed in Kinmel Camp. Firstly, they were accused of stealing quantities of jam, sardines and peas from Messrs. Melia's, and secondly for stealing quantities of tobacco and cigarettes from the YMCA hut. Superintendent A. E. Lindsay made an application for the two to be remanded in custody for further enquiries to be made into these matters, which was granted by the magistrate.

Stealing and Receiving

In the last week of August 1917, two youths appeared in court before the St Asaph Magistrates. Frederick Davies, aged fourteen, a milk boy of the Water Works, Glascoed, near St Asaph, and William Kerfoot, aged sixteen of Marli Farm, Cefn, near St Asaph, were found guilty of the offences of stealing and receiving two boxes of cigarettes from a canteen at Kinmel Camp. They were bound over for twelve months and ordered to pay 16s 6d costs.

Burglaries on Successive Nights

The *Abergele and Pensarn Visitor* of 1 December 1917 carried this short piece:

> On two recent nights in succession, a lock-up shop belonging to an Abergele firm located close to Kinmel Camp, has been broken into by burglars. On each occasion food was taken away from a store cupboard. Entry was gained by the breaking of a window. Each time the burglar left behind a pair of steps, which he used to reach the window.

Guilty of Theft

In early January of 1918, Mary Agnes Williams of 7, Rhuddlan Road, Abergele, appeared before the local Magistrates Court charged with theft. She was accused of the theft of a number of garments belonging to a Miss M. Owen, a cook at the military hospital in No.10 Camp, at Kinmel Camp. Mary Agnes Williams was found guilty of theft and was fined £1 13s 0d, including costs. She was supposed to have delivered a parcel of clothing to someone in Abergele, but instead kept the items.

Woman Deserter makes Allegations

The *Liverpool Echo* of Thursday, 17 January 1918, carried this somewhat intriguing article:

WOMAN DESERTER
ALLEGATIONS AGAINST MEN IN TRAINING
CAMP

Fanny Burgess, the daughter of an Audenshaw labourer, was charged under the Defence of the Realm Act [known as DORA], at Ashton, yesterday, with being an absentee from the Women's Army Auxiliary Corps, at Kinmel Park.

Burgess, who appeared in the uniform of the Corps, said, 'If I had not come home I should have done away with myself. It was miserable there. There was no fire or comfort, and we were not allowed to light a fire until half- past- five. The boys at Kinmel were different from Oswestry. We were never insulted at Kinmel'.

She made grave allegations against the male members of staff at Oswestry, to which camp the authorities at Kinmel had threatened to send her again.

Superintendent Carson said that inquiries were being conducted into accusations made by Burgess and seven other girls.

Before the hearing was concluded, Burgess fell in a faint, and was carried out of court by two police officers. It was some time before she recovered.

The magistrates adjourned the case for fourteen days and in the meantime asked that the police should communicate with the authorities, pointing out that the magistrates felt that at present Burgess was not physically fit to do the work.

Fanny Burgess did not much like Kinmel Camp, but she most certainly abhorred the military Camp at Oswestry and certain male members of staff there.

Drummer Boys' Theft at Kinmel Park Camp
Before the Rhyl Police Court in late February of 1918, appeared three drummer boys from Kinmel Camp. At the court, Thomas Egan, aged sixteen, Leslie Fairclough, aged fifteen and Thomas Lycett, aged seventeen, pleaded guilty to stealing a postal packet containing a wrist watch, a cake and some sweets, the property of John Gaunt, a fellow drummer boy at the camp, who at the time of the offence was a patient in the camp's military hospital. The three stole the postal packet and its contents from a hut at Kinmel Camp and shared out the contents between them. Captain and Adjutant Willis, M.C., told the police court that he was unable to speak well of any of the three miscreants, who had caused a lot of trouble at the camp since their arrival, but were too young to be court martialled!

Thomas Egan admitted that he had been 'birched' in Ireland and had also been involved in Sinn Fein activities in Ireland. The magistrates decided to give the three youths a chance, due to their ages. They were bound over for twelve months and ordered to pay between them 22s 10d costs.

Prosecutions for Profiteering in Wartime
At St Asaph Petty Sessions in early April 1918 three shopkeepers with shop premises on the very outskirts of Kinmel Park Camp were prosecuted for profiteering in wartime.

George Parry Roberts, the Shop and Restaurant Rooms, opposite Kinmel Camp, was charged with selling one pound of blackcurrant jam at 1s 2d, instead of at 1s per pound – the maximum permitted under wartime pricing regulations. Mr

Joseph Lloyd told the court that the regulations were framed to prevent profiteering and to protect the poor who could not afford the high prices. In the case of Mr G P Roberts' shop opposite the camp, the customers usually were soldiers and they could ill afford the 'extra price', as he put it. A witness for the prosecution, Private Evelyn Kerr, a WAAC in the camp, said that the defendant charged her 1s 2d for one pound of blackcurrant jam. The defendant replied that he had bought the jam at 1s 1d per pound in July of 1917 and he considered that 1s 2d per pound 'was not a heavy price'. It was also his first sale that day after getting up! Mr Roberts was also accused of selling bread for more than the permitted 2¼d per pound. Private Kerr told the court that she had paid 5d for a 2 pound loaf. The defendant said he had charged her only 4½d, the extra ½d being for the wrapper and bag for wrapping up the bread. In reply Private Kerr said she did not ask for a bag or paper, and she saw no notice in the shop that a halfpenny was charged for a wrapper or bag.

Mr Roberts also denied that he had offered the Inspector who attended at his shop 10s if he overlooked the case! The defendant also broke the regulations by failing to display the required price list prominently in his shop premises. He was found guilty of the three charges (the alleged 10s bribe being set aside), and the Magistrates stated that they were 'determined to stop the profiteering'. Mr Roberts was fined heavily – £2 in each case, plus £2 2s advocate's fee and 5s 'allowance' to Private Kerr. In all, a very hefty fine of £12 11s.

At the same court, Elisabeth Jones, shopkeeper, Bodelwyddan, pleaded guilty to selling two pounds of strawberry and apple jam at 2s, instead of the permitted maximum of 1s 5½d for two pounds. She was also fined for not displaying the required list of prices prominently in her shop. Her fine was £8 9s.

A third defendant, Mr Domenico Sidoli of Rhyl, who had a shop premises opposite No 7 Camp in Kinmel Camp, also pleaded guilty to like offences, though pleaded ignorance of them. He was also fined £8 9s.

Shocking Shooting and Killing of a Young Soldier: Manslaughter or Murder?
The 4 May 1918 edition of the *Abergele and Pensarn Visitor* gave an early and only brief report of a shocking incident that had occurred at Kinmel Camp. It was the first report locally of this matter:

> At Kinmel Camp on Wednesday night, a Private in the Manchester Regiment who was detained in the Guardroom, had with him his rifle and a ball cartridge which he is alleged to have fired through a ventilator into a group of young soldiers. The bullet passed through the body of one Private and embedded itself in the body of another. The men were taken to the camp hospital where one died and where the other is in a critical condition.

In the following week's edition of the newspaper much more information on this matter had come into the public domain. The *Abergele and Pensarn Advertiser* published this article concerning the inquest into the death of Private John Victor Hawkins:

> THE KINMEL PARK TRAGEDY
> Some hours were taken up by an Inquest at Kinmel Park on Friday evening, held by Mr J. Roberts Jones, the Deputy Coroner for Flintshire, touching upon the death of Private John Victor Hawkins, aged eighteen, of Heywood, Lancashire.

Evidence was given that at about 7.15 p.m. on May 1, whilst a number of soldiers were gathered around the Battalion notice board at No. 20 Camp, a rifle shot rang out and Hawkins fell wounded in the breast and expired almost immediately. Another soldier named Grindley was wounded at the same time. In a cell of the Guardroom 130 yards away Private John Jenner was found lying in a restless state on the floor. After being searched he admitted that he had fired the rifle found in the cell through the ventilator. The rifle was clean, but had the smell of burnt powder about it. While in Jenner's haversack a warm discharged cartridge was found. Through the ventilator a clear view of the spot where Hawkins fell could be had. There was no knowledge that Jenner and Hawkins knew each other or that there had been 'any bad blood' between them, and anyone else in the camp. Jenner was undergoing 95 hours Detention, which had commenced on Monday.

Questions were asked as to how Jenner came to be in possession of a rifle and service ammunition in the cell. It was stated that it was part of the duty of the person in charge of the Prisoner to search him before he was placed in confinement and to take away such things if found, from him. In this instance someone had been guilty of a breach of a very important regulation and the man who had handed Jenner the rifle had been placed under arrest for neglecting his duty. It was most irregular for a Prisoner to have a rifle and ammunition in his cell, although under Detention a man had to go through drills with his Company and keep his equipment in order.

Captain Dr Dalton of the Royal Army Medical Corps described the wounds inflicted on Hawkins by the bullet and attributed death to haemorrhage and shock. Private Hamer said that he was standing shoulder to shoulder with Hawkins, in front of the notice board at the moment he was shot. He heard the shot and at the same moment Hawkins shouted, 'Oh, I'm shot' and then fell on his back.

Jenner was present throughout the enquiry and was quite lively in his demeanour, but he chose not to give any evidence himself or to ask questions of any of the witnesses.

The Jury returned a Verdict of Manslaughter against Jenner and added a rider to the effect that there was great neglect in allowing Jenner to have a rifle and cartridge in his cell.

Private John Jenner was brought before Dr Peter Jones, Messrs. Edward Williams and H.E. Prichard at Abergele Police Court on Monday and was Charged with the Manslaughter of Private John Victor Hawkins. No evidence was offered, with the accused being Remanded until Monday next.

The following week after this inquest, it was reported that Private John Jenner had been indicted for the manslaughter of Private John Victor Hawkins. by shooting him at Kinmel Camp, and was again brought before the Abergele bench on Monday morning and was further remanded.

The following week's edition of the *Abergele and Pensarn Advertiser* (25 May 1918) carried this further article:

GRAVE CHARGE AGAINST A YOUNG SOLDIER FOR THE WILFUL MURDER OF JOHN VICTOR HAWKINS OF THE SAME REGIMENT AND WITH DOING GRIEVOUS BODILY HARM TO PRIVATE JOHN GRINDLEY

Private Albert George Hansen, a native of Cardiff was
charged with being an accessory before and after the
fact.

Both prisoners are mere youths being just turned
eighteen and Jenner being a native of London.

Subsequently no Prima Facie case was proved against
Hansen and he was Discharged. Whilst Jenner
received only Twelve Months Imprisonment with
Hard Labour after being found guilty by the Jury of
Manslaughter by a Reckless Act.

I thought having read the facts surrounding this case that
Private John Jenner had got off very lightly in receiving only
one year's imprisonment with hard labour. To my
astonishment I found that on 3 July 1918, in the Court of
Appeal before Justices Darling, Rowlatt and Sankey, John
Jenner was appealing against his conviction at Ruthin
Assizes of manslaughter and his having been sentenced to
the twelve months imprisonment with hard labour. Mr
Artemus Jones represented the appellant, John Jenner and
Sir Ellis Griffith KC, appeared for the prosecution.

The facts surrounding the case were again given, but at
this appeal, Mr Artemus Jones gave John Jenner's version of
events. They were that he had been placed in the guardroom
from the Monday to the Wednesday and on the latter day he
had been sent to do certain work near a trench. He had been
chewing cordite and was taken ill as a result. Sitting down
near the trench he discovered a live cartridge, which he put
into his pocket. He was then returned to his guardroom cell
and found that his rifle and equipment had been placed
there for him to clean. With nothing else for him to do in the
cell he practised loading and unloading his rifle with the
cartridge that he had found near the trench. In order to do
this he rested the rifle in a ventilator in the cell, he being a

weak youth of eighteen and unable to hold it for any length of time. Whilst doing this and pulling the safety plug on the rifle back with his thumbs, he involuntarily touched the trigger with his finger and that caused the rifle to go off. The bullet killed a Soldier named Hawkins and wounded another soldier.

Mr Artemus Jones stated the grounds for the Appeal were that Justice Bray in his Summing Up to the Ruthin Assizes Jury had not adequately explained to them the point of Criminal Negligence. In fact, Justice Bray's Summing Up was so inadequate as to have misled the Jury.

Mr Justice Darling on behalf of the Appeal Court stated, 'A more unlikely story than that of the prisoner Jenner, he had never heard in his life.'

Mr Artemus Jones rose and pointed out that the Ruthin Assizes Jury had believed Jenner.

Mr Justice Darling came back curtly with, 'Did they? As he was only eighteen they might not have considered convicting him of Murder.'

The Appeal was dismissed with Justice Darling adding, 'Juries are reluctant to convict young persons of Murder and take every opportunity to avoid convicting them of so serious a charge.' He concluded proceedings by stating, 'The prisoner was very lucky indeed not have been found guilty of Murder.'

John Victor Hawkins, Private, Regimental Number 95021 was buried at Heywood Cemetery, Rochdale Road East, Heywood, Lancashire.

Alleged Assault on the Kinmel Camp Railway

Before H. E. Prichard, Edward Williams and John Pierce at a special sitting of the Abergele magistrates on Tuesday morning, 7 May 1918, was Sapper George F. Brown of the Royal Engineers, attached to 53rd Battalion, the Cheshire

Regiment, presently at Kinmel Camp. He was brought into court and charged with committing an indecent assault upon Margaret Jones, a cook employed in the 'Navy and Army' at Kinmel Camp. The indecent assault having allegedly taken place on 22 April 1918, on the 10.30 p.m. late return train from Rhyl to Kinmel Camp.

The prosecution evidence given was that Margaret Jones was in an empty compartment of the train when the accused Brown entered her compartment and first asked for her ticket, purporting to be a railway employee. He then asked if he could travel with her in the compartment. He then was alleged to have forcibly kissed her, pushed her down in her seat and assaulted her. She struggled against his unwanted attentions and told him several times to stop and that she would report him to the authorities. Sapper George F. Brown was committed to the next Quarter Sessions.

Despite the fact that Margaret Jones was said to have been a good worker and of exemplary character, and had reported the 'assault' promptly to a senior officer at Kinmel Camp, the jury deliberated for only twelve minutes before returning a verdict of not guilty. With no known witnesses to the 'alleged assault' the jury did not convict Sapper Brown.

One that nearly got away!
The *Merthyr Pioneer* of 8 June 1918 informed of a man who was a sort of cross between a Conscientious Objector and what they called then a 'skulker':

C.O. Fined at Rhyl
At Rhyl last Friday, Leonard Simpson, described as a warehouseman of Higher Green, Astley, Lancashire, was fined £2 and handed over to a military escort as an absentee under the Military Service Act. It was

stated that he was posted to the Army on January 13 1917, but nothing more was heard of him until he was handed over by the Civil Police at Kinmel Camp on Thursday.

He said he had a conscientious objection to combatant service, but had offered himself for RAMC work. He declined to state where he had been since January of last year.

Leonard Simpson had done rather well to keep a very low profile for some seventeen months in order to avoid his official call-up for military service. He was indeed – one that nearly got away!

Stealing of Beer

At the Rhyl Police Court on Thursday, 12 December 1918, a Canadian soldier based at Kinmel Camp named Robert John Ritchie appeared to answer a charge of stealing. He was alleged to have stolen beer from casks on the railway track at Kinmel Camp. He admitted to having taken the beer but contended that he did not know that it was stolen when he was handed it by another man. He was found guilty and committed to prison for one month. Ritchie immediately gave notice that he would appeal against his conviction and the prison sentence imposed upon him. The magistrates released Ritchie on bail in order that he could obtain legal assistance for the drawing up of his appeal in writing.

However, on Monday, 16 December 1918, the Rhyl magistrates were informed that Ritchie had decided not to proceed with his appeal and he had surrendered himself to undergo his prison sentence. Was it perhaps that Kinmel Camp was so awful that prison held little or no fears for a soldier such as Ritchie, who may well have seen some active service at the Front?

Yet Another Kinmel Park Camp Bigamist!

This case of bigamy involved a corporal and a member of the Women's Army Auxiliary Corps (WAAC) who were both stationed at Kinmel Camp.

At Rhyl Magistrates Court in Christmas week of 1918, before Mr T. D. Jones and Mr B. Wadsworth, was a Corporal Sidney Edward Doney, otherwise known as Sidney Edward Lobb, of 53rd Young Soldiers Battalion, the Cheshire Regiment, stationed in No.1 Camp at Kinmel Camp. Corporal Doney/Lobb was charged with bigamy. One of the witnesses against him was Mrs Henrietta Lobb of 3, Peel Road, St Hellier, Jersey, who told the court that on 30 March 1913, at St.Hellier, Jersey, she married the accused. There had been two children from their marriage, a boy and a girl, but the former had died. She had last seen her husband, the accused, in April 1918, when he had been home on six days' leave.

Ernest Alfred Channing then gave evidence. He was a drummer in the Jersey Garrison and a brother of Mrs Henrietta Lobb. He gave evidence that he was present at the 1913 marriage of his sister and the accused and he pointed in court at the accused, starkly identifying him as his brother-in-law, known to him as Sidney Edward Lobb!

Beatrice May Dunford of home address, 48, Birch Grove, Nant-y-Bwlch, Tredegar, south Wales, then gave her evidence. She stated that she joined the Women's Army Auxiliary Corps (WAAC) and for the past nine months had been stationed at Kinmel Camp. About a fortnight after arriving at Kinmel Camp, she became acquainted with the accused who told her from the outset that his name was Sidney Edward Lobb. The couple got engaged and when the banns were read at Bodelwyddan Church the accused then told her that his surname was actually Doney. She remembered that when she first met him she said jokingly to him, 'Where is your wife?', and he replied, 'I have got no wife. I would not have asked you to come for a walk if I had got a wife'. She questioned him about the new surname he gave her of Doney; he explained this by saying that the name Lobb was because his mother had married again, but that he had been baptised in the name of Doney. The accused and Beatrice May Dunford were 'married' on 13 November 1918.

On 10 December 1918, she received information that he had previously been married, and was, in the eyes of the law, still married, to someone else! She confronted him, but he denied the allegation.

Deputy Chief Constable Lindsay gave evidence that on that same day, 10 December 1918, the accused Doney/Lobb was taken into police custody and he was charged with the offence of bigamy. That day he continued to deny the charge, but on the following day he volunteered a further statement admitting his guilt.

Giving evidence in his own defence to the court, the accused said that his wife Henrietta did not love him. Also that he had been now in the army for going on seventeen years, having first joined the Devonshire Regiment. He produced to the court a Certificate of Good Character from the army. He then applied for a certificate under the Poor Prisoners Act for legal aid, which was granted. He was committed to be tried at the next Flintshire Assizes.

5

Some Longer Stories

The 'Dishonourable' Gentleman
The strange case of the Honourable (a debatable title for this particular man) Charles William Joseph Henry Blake, the eldest son of the Irish Peer, Lord Wallscourt (the 4th Baron Wallscourt, Erroll Augustus Blake). C. W. J. H. Blake was a Second Lieutenant with 12th Battalion, the Royal Welch Fusiliers, when on 28 August 1915, at Kinmel Camp he was found to be in a drunken state whilst on duty. Lieutenant Blake admitted the offence and there and then was given the opportunity to resign his Commission with immediate effect or be placed under arrest. Second Lieutenant Blake claimed that he had in fact already sent in an application to resign his commission and he was ordered to remain for the time being at the camp. However, he chose to leave the camp later the same day and was on the evening of 8 September 1915, taken into police custody by a PC Rooney at Wilton Road, Pimlico, London, having been found staggering across the road and narrowly avoiding being hit by an omnibus.

On 15 September 1915, an army escort was sent to London to return the disgraced Second Lieutenant Blake to his Battalion at Kinmel Camp. He had already appeared at a London Police Court for the offence committed on 8 September 1915.

Then on Tuesday, 12 October 1915, Second Lieutenant Blake appeared before a court martial at Kinmel Camp and he pleaded guilty to the military charge of being absent without leave. The accused admitted to being in the habit of taking too much drink and that he could not stop himself 'craving for drink', as he put it himself. He stated that he had been urged by others not to apply for a commission, but when he had found that nearly all his friends had joined the army, he felt somewhat compelled to do so himself. The accused had also hoped that military service would enable him to pull himself together, but instead he found the physical exertions too much for him and he remained unable to avoid stimulants. He further claimed that he had submitted an application to resign his Commission, but that for whatever reason it had not been forwarded to Battalion Headquarters and that he only had a hazy recollection of being ordered to remain in the camp.

Surprisingly, the court martial found him not guilty of the charge of being absent without leave, and stated that their decision on the charge of drunkenness would be announced at a later date. Nothing of course to do with this 'Hooray Henry' being a member of the upper echelons of society! The lengths to which the authorities went in order to 'press gang' genuine Conscientious Objectors into the Military, was, of course, in stark contrast with their easy acquiescence for 'The Honourable' C. W. J. H. Blake to just walk away from his requirement to serve in the military!

The German Doctor(s) Story – Alleged Poisoning of Soldiers

The German Doctor(s) Story first broke 'openly in public' in the House of Commons on 28 June 1916, though it had been a major topic of conversation in and around Kinmel Camp for some weeks. It had already taken on all the fine trappings of an apocryphal story, one that even today is still believed by many, especially by some descendants of soldiers who were at the camp at the relevant time. Hansard reports that Athelstan Rendall, the well-respected Member of Parliament for Thornbury, Gloucestershire, at the

Commons Military Service Sitting, asked the Secretary of State for War a quite startling question, though one that had been submitted in writing prior to this Sitting:

> Athelstan Rendall: 'Whether two Doctors in the employ of the Army have since been found to be Germans and have been proved to have administered drugs of a poisonous nature to Soldier's attending at a camp in Wales. With fatal results in some cases'.

> Mr Tennant, the Financial Secretary to the War Office replied on behalf of the Secretary of State for War: 'I have no information of the kind suggested and my medical advisors consider the story to have no basis other than imagination'.

So now this 'story' was out in the public domain. Athelstan Rendall MP (1871–1948) asked many relevant and important war-related parliamentary questions during the period, many of them concerning the treatment of soldiers, their medical needs and requirements. Newspapers now had this story of the German Doctor(s) and rumours relating to it were being spread ever more widely, particularly by the soldiers leaving Kinmel Camp to move to other military camps or to the Front, meant the 'camp in Wales' was soon revealed to be Kinmel Camp, where a number of shall we say, suspicious deaths of soldiers had taken place in the first four or so months of 1916.

The *Liverpool Daily Post* amongst others keenly followed the story and ran with it. Their Thursday 15 July 1916 edition carried this story of a further exchange in the House of Commons:

A Kinmel Park Canard – Extraordinary Crop of Errors

Mr Athelstan Rendall, the Liberal MP for Thornbury asked the Secretary of State for War a number of questions. Whether a Doctor Speirs was for some time attached in the capacity of a Doctor to Kinmel Park, Wales? Whether he was aware that his name did not appear in the Register of British Medical Practitioners and that he was said to have been German speaking with a German accent and with German sympathies? Whether he subsequently went to the Front and if he was now dead, what was the cause of death?

Rumours abounded that this alleged German doctor (or doctors), had been executed in some manner as a result of the evil deeds carried out at Kinmel Camp. Also that his/their body/bodies had been secretly buried in the nearby St Margaret's churchyard, Bodelwyddan.

Mr Tennant had now moved on in July 1916, much probably to his relief for a variety of good reasons, to become the new Secretary for Scotland. His successor as Financial Secretary to the War Office, Mr Henry Forster, replied to these questions, stating that Lieutenant H. Speirs had been employed at Kinmel Park Camp from January 17 until April 3 1916 and that his name could be found in the Medical Register as MB CH, Edinburgh, MD, FRCS, Edinburgh. He was recommended for a Temporary Commission in the Royal Army Medical Corps (RAMC) by the Scottish Medical Services Emergency Committee. That there was no reason to think that Lieutenant H. Speirs had German sympathies; he was on active service with the RAMC in France.

Mr Rendall was not prepared to let this matter go and

then asked whether the Senior Medical Officer at Kinmel Camp had lately resigned his post and if so, whether he did so because he was tired of being worried with questions about the alleged German doctor at Kinmel Camp.

Mr Forster said in reply that Captain G. L. Travis had been appointed Sanitary Officer to Kinmel Camp on May 7 and that to date he still held that appointment. He added that no officer who has been in medical charge of Kinmel Park had resigned his post. The present incumbent was said to have held the appointment for some months, his predecessor having been relieved on account of ill-health.

These allegations and revelations becoming public knowledge, and being in some quarters believed as being true, came at a most difficult time for the British government and the War Office. The war was not going well for Britain and its Allies, and the Easter Rising in Ireland a few weeks earlier was having serious repercussions.

My own father-in-law, Mr Thomas David (TD) Jones of Henllan, near Denbigh, Denbighshire, well remembers his own late Father, Thomas Jones, who trained at Kinmel Camp in 1916, with 9th Battalion, the South Wales Borderers, telling him the story of a German doctor killing soldiers at Kinmel Camp by poisoning them. Thomas Jones was stationed at Kinmel Camp during the relevant period, before being sent to Mesopotamia with a draft of soldiers from his Battalion.

Looking back now some 100 years, without any hard evidence coming to light, we can only speculate as to the truth of this German doctor(s) story. I find it most strange that Dr Henry Speirs, a Scottish-born doctor, no doubt with a Scottish accent of some kind being taken for a German and for having German sympathies! Only his surname of 'Speirs' could be misconstrued as being Germanic. Was this Dr Henry Speirs pushed forward as a scapegoat for a real

German doctor or doctors at Kinmel Camp? Perhaps the doctor or doctors had German-sounding accents or were from another European country.

For my own part I believe that several of the soldiers' deaths between January and April of 1916 were somewhat suspicious. I offer a possible explanation that these deaths were the result of a 'cocktail' of vaccinations and inoculations administered to the soldiers at Kinmel Camp, some of the vaccines being in their early stages of development. Just a few had a seriously adverse reaction to what they received and not all of them. But this is, of course, just my theory. At least two of those who died were apparently very well until a few short days after they were vaccinated at Kinmel Camp.

The War Diary and Life of George John Culpitt

George John Culpitt was born on 22 April 1897, at Noel Street, Islington, London, being the first-born son of George Thomas Culpitt, then an artificial flower commercial traveller, and his wife, Rachel Sarah Culpitt (nee Picton). On Empire Day in 1909, when he was a pupil at Ecclesbourne Road School, Islington, George John Culpitt recalled his headmaster in an address to the school prophetically stating that 'Germany was the enemy and that not many years would elapse before we should come to grips'. We know of this quote as it was in a young George John Culpitt's diary. All his life he was a great diary-keeper and for this we owe him our gratitude, especially for his wonderful diary account of his own experiences during the Great War.

George was seventeen when he was actually in the crowd outside Buckingham Palace on the night of 4 August 1914, the day that Britain declared war on Germany. The crowd sang such songs as 'God Save the King', 'God Bless the

Prince of Wales' and even the French National Anthem 'La Marseillaise'. There followed 1,566 days of war, resulting in death and misery for millions. Happily George's two younger brothers, William Robert Culpitt, born 1900 and Arthur Picton Culpitt, born 1902, were too young to face the horrors of the First World War.

George John Culpitt became one of Lord Kitchener's Volunteer Army when he enlisted on 6 December 1915 in 3rd Battalion, the Royal Welch Fusiliers, (because he had a Welsh-born friend who was joining this Regiment at the time). George was sent in early 1916, to undergo military training at Kinmel Camp, so far from this eighteen–year-old's family and roots in London. This is an extract from Private Culpitt's opening chapter: it makes interesting reading relating to Kinmel Camp:

Chapter 1 – Into France
At length after we had returned from our meagre leave we were officially warned for the Front and then began the various preparations such as drawing kit etc, which every draft had to undergo.

Swiftly the days passed and at last came April 27 1916, that day being the one on which we were to leave Kinmel Park for France.

We were treated to a good feed in the canteen which commenced at 3.30 p.m. and presented by the Proprietors with a bag containing 1/- of assorted stuff. Our Captain also gave us a box of 50 cigarettes each and we also received various other boxes of fags. Rations for two days in the form of bread, cheese, cake etc. were also dished out and the puzzle was where to put all the stuff we received.

Having made our farewells we fell in and marched out of the canteen and were joined by the Band and the rest of the Battalion that was accompanying us to the station. On arrival at Abergele the town turned out to give us a cheer as was the custom as we entered the station. During the short wait for the train that ensued, the Band played popular aires, but the train soon pulled into the platform and we boarded it and made ourselves comfortable: but we only went as far as Crewe, for here we were to catch a troop train that would take us right through to the coast.

Thomas Jones of Groes, near Denbigh – Bayoneted but Survived

My wife's paternal Taid, Thomas Jones, whom you will also find on the dedication page of this book, was born on 21 February 1892 at Groes, near Denbigh, Denbighshire, to Thomas Jones (senior), born in Henllan, near Denbigh, and his Trawsfynydd-born wife, Mary. His mother, Mary Jones died when he was a young child and he found himself being somewhat passed around various relatives for his nurturing. So it was no surprise that 'our' Thomas Jones decided to seek a different life for himself and he attested and enlisted on 17 May 1916, in the South Wales Borderers. He was firstly placed with 9th Battalion and sent for his initial military training with them to Kinmel Camp. His arrival coincided with the tail end of the German doctor(s) story', and whilst he was at the camp the story was spoken of in The House of Commons and reported upon in the British press.

When the time came in late summer 1916 for Thomas Jones to be sent out with a draft overseas he was transferred to 4th Battalion, the South Wales Borderers, and marched with his comrades to Rhyl railway station to embark on a troop train. However, once at Rhyl railway station an officer on horseback rode up and called out his name and regimental number for him to fall out and to return 'at the double' to Kinmel Camp, with all his army equipment. So he marched all the way back 'at the double' as he would later do, accompanied by the officer on horseback and it was only once back at Kinmel Camp that he was informed of the reason for being called back to camp: his father had died. He was granted three days compassionate leave.

Thomas returned to camp three days later after the burial of his father and was sent out with the next draft of 4th Battalion, the South Wales Borderers to Mesopotamia. Like so many of these soldiers he did not over the years speak much of what he had been through and then only when asked a direct question. We do know that he was on a boat ferrying soldiers to the shore when it was sunk by Turkish shellfire from the mainland. Thomas Jones could not swim but he and many comrades survived by hanging on in the water to large pieces of flotsam and jetsam until they were rescued and brought ashore.

Thomas Jones served in Mesopotamia and in Egypt with 4th Battalion and he brought home with him from the War a pith helmet he had worn during his Middle East War Service. It was played with for many years by his children and then later by his grandchildren, but sadly was lost sometime in the last few years.

What we can be certain of is that he was badly bayoneted on the left side of his face by an enemy soldier, which left a long nasty-looking scar down his face. When asked many years ago by his son, my dear father-in-law, Thomas David (TD) Jones about this, he said that he was saved from a probably fatal wound by the bayonet hitting his cheekbone. He also survived being 'finished off' by the enemy soldier, as one of his comrades 'did for him', as he put it. This was hand-to-hand fighting. For the rest of his life the left side of his face would cause him great pain in cold weather, and would 'flare up' and look very nasty. When he had applied for some kind of army pension or payment for this war-related injury he was refused. On the top of his head red marks could clearly be seen, which were actually pieces of embedded shrapnel. These war-gained marks seemed not to worry him, but fascinated his grandchildren, whose father banned them from ever asking their grandfather about them.

But what Thomas Jones would say freely to his son over the years, was that the German doctor story was true: that a German doctor at Kinmel Camp had poisoned and killed a number of British soldiers in training there. That is one of the reasons that the camp gained the names of 'Kill'em Park' and the like. He said it with complete belief, and also said that many soldiers at the camp at the time also knew and believed the truth of the story.

Albert Nevitt, MC and Albert Medal – a Hero from North Wales

Albert Nevitt, a young teacher, attested and enlisted in the war in 10th Battalion, the Royal Welch Fusiliers, as a Private. He received his Commission to become an officer after applying in writing, and was made a Temporary Second Lieutenant with effect from 24 January 1915, with 12th Battalion, the Royal Welch Fusiliers. After passing through officer training he was sent to France on 31 March 1916.

The *London Gazette*, Issue 29584, of 16 May 1916, has the following under this general heading:

> His Majesty the King has been graciously pleased to confer the Military Cross on the under mentioned officers and Warrant Officers, in recognition of their gallantry and devotion to duty in the field.

This was the Citation for Albert Nevitt:

Temp. 2nd Lt. Albert Nevitt, 12Bn (formerly 10 Bn) R.W. Fus

For conspicuous gallantry when leading a bombing attack upon a communication trench all but one of his men became casualties, but with this man he went on to within 10 yards of the enemy, when he was himself wounded. He had previously shown great daring on reconnaissance.

Albert Nevitt was returned to these shores from the Front in France. He was, by September of 1916, a Lieutenant temporarily attached to 62nd Training Reserve Battalion at Kinmel Camp. Unsurprisingly, due to his exploits at the Front involving 'bombing attacks' with grenades and bombs, he found himself as one of the Instructors at the camp's Bombing and Grenade School. It was here that things for him became more difficult even than when on an attack on the enemy at the Front!

Three serious incidents occurred at Kinmel Camp during the period of September and October 1916, which truly required all the guts, determination and complete disregard for his own safety that he had already shown in his actions in France. The *London Gazette*, Issue 30457 of 4 January 1918 provides us with the salient details of two of the incidents which resulted in his being now awarded the rare Albert Medal:

Lieutenant Albert Nevitt, M.C., Royal Welsh Fusiliers.

On the 4 September, 1916, bombing instruction was taking place in a trench occupied by Lieutenant (then Second Lieutenant) Nevitt, another officer, and two men. One of the men threw a bomb which hit the parapet, and fell back into the trench, where it was deeply embedded in mud and water. Lieutenant Nevitt at once groped for the bomb. He failed to find it at the first attempt, but made a second and successful attempt, seized the bomb, and threw it over the parapet, where it at once exploded.

On the 24th September 1916 bombing instruction was taking place under the command of Lieutenant Nevitt. Another officer and three men were present in the trench. A bomb fell back from the parapet into the trench, whereupon the men rushed for the entrance, nearly knocking Lieutenant Nevitt down. In the confusion Lieutenant Nevitt lost sight of the bomb, but he searched for it, and, having found it, threw it clear, when it at once exploded. Only one of the men had succeeded in escaping from the trench when the bomb exploded.

On both occasions Lieutenant Nevitt's courage and presence of mind undoubtedly saved the lives of others.

But that was not quite the end of it, as on 4 October 1916 at Kinmel Camp, there was an explosion in a bomb store and despite the high risk of further explosions occurring, Lieutenant Nevitt stayed in the bomb store to render assistance to an injured sergeant. This incident was not even included in the citation for his Albert Medal award.

On 21 March 1918 he was promoted from his then rank of Lieutenant (and Acting Captain and Adjutant) to Temporary Captain. This occurred when he was for a time with the King's Royal Lancashire Regiment. He somehow managed to survive the war and returning home to north Wales, he went back to teaching. During the inter-war years he became the headmaster of Deganwy School.

The *North Wales Weekly News* of Thursday, 11 August 1966, contained this obituary piece upon Albert Nevitt, which included but little some details of his fine military career, but most certainly not all of it, as it omitted to make mention of his having been awarded the Albert Medal:

Former Deganwy Headmaster – Death of Mr Albert Nevitt

Mr Albert Nevitt of Gannoc Court, Deganwy, who died on Thursday aged 73, was the Headmaster of Deganwy School for 33 years until his retirement. A native of Conway Borough, he was the son of Alderman and Mrs Henry Nevitt of Llandudno Junction. He was a Captain in the R.W. Fusiliers during the 1914–1918 War and won the M.C. In the Second World War he was Commissioned in the RAF. Mr Nevitt was Vicar's Warden of Llanrhos Parish and was Treasurer of the All Saints Church, Deganwy for 27 years. He was a Past Master of the Lodge of St Tudno.

I found these two rather nice little pieces relating to Albert Nevitt the head teacher and man, rather than Albert Nevitt the soldier and war hero. They were on a blog relating to the history of Deganwy School with contributions from past pupils including these two:

1) 'I recall on my first day at school that I cried my heart out in class all morning and our Headmaster Mr Nevitt kept coming into our Infants Class to try and get me to stop crying, but I would not. I can clearly remember him forever calling me by my Father's name every time he came in. I think Mr Nevitt also taught my Father during the 1930's in the Old School

down by the Church House'. My parents took me back to school at lunchtime, but Mr Nevitt would not take me back until the following year.

2) In Ysgol Deganwy it was Mr Nevitt and Mr Illyd Williams who were great mentors.

David B. Milne, an Official Canadian War Artist at Kinmel Park Camp

David Brown Milne, the Canadian-born artist (painter), printmaker and writer, better known as David B. Milne, was born on 8 January 1882, in his family's log cabin at Burgoyne, Saugeen Township, Ontario, Canada. He was the last-born of ten children of William Milne and his wife, Mary, who had emigrated to Canada in 1880 from Aberdeenshire. At aged eight, David B. Milne moved with his family to the village of Paisley, Elderslie Township, Bruce County, Ontario, Canada.

David B. Milne was educated until the age of ten by his stern Presbyterian mother, who taught him that spiritual ideals were better than material goals. The Milne family were poor and only two of their ten children, one of them being David, even got to complete their high school education. David was said to have been very bright at school and from about 1900 to 1903, he taught at the United School, a small country school near Paisley, Elderslie Township. He then went to study art at the highly regarded Art Students League art school in New York between 1903 and 1905. David Milne had boldly taken a gigantic step as a young man by moving to Manhattan, New York, to study art and there to support himself financially. Once his money saved from teaching had gone, he made posters, showcards and illustrated stories for magazines to help make ends meet.

Around 1909, David Milne realised that he really wanted to be an artist, a painter, not an illustrator. He is quoted as having once said that, 'Painting, is a drawing made readable'. His paintings sparingly use colour.

He married Mary Frances (known as Patsy) Hegarty in 1912, and in 1916 they moved out of Manhattan to a more rustic and hilly area of New York known as Boston Corners.

He had earlier, in New York, met a man who was to be a good friend to him for many years: James Clarke, an artist himself who had chosen to work in advertising in the city rather than become an artist/painter, which could often take you on the road to misery and poverty. James Clarke would on occasions lend David Milne money and was later to assist his career in a very big way.

In 1917, when residing at Boston Corners, Columbia County, New York, the United States declared war on Germany and its fellow Central Powers allies. Probably because he faced being drafted into the United States military, David Milne returned home to Canada and enlisted in the Canadian Army. He was enrolled at Toronto on 1 March 1918, in 2nd Depot Battalion, 1st Central Ontario Regiment. Though Milne was something of an artist already, he was little known. According to legend as they say, Milne's first military duty was to shovel coal in severe weather during an emergency at the Western Hospital, Toronto. Milne spent the Summer of 1918 in Canada, undergoing military training, before, in September 1918, leaving Canada for Europe and the ongoing war.

The military records relating to Milne are difficult to fully fathom. Though shown on the strength of 8th Reserve Infantry Battalion which was based in Southern England, he was actually receiving his Canadian Army Pay on 1 October 1918, for being stationed at Kinmel Camp, north Wales. He remained at Kinmel Camp until at least 28 January 1919.

For some four months Milne became a permanent member of the Canadian contingent at Kinmel Camp, which in late autumn of 1918 and pre-Armistice (11 November 1918) was being used as a training camp for a Canadian Young Soldier's Battalion, as a segregation camp for the quarantine of incoming drafts of men from Canada against infectious diseases and for drafts to receive further training and be 'kitted out' before being moved out to the training Battalions in southern England. Post-Armistice, Kinmel Camp for Canadian soldiers became nothing more than a holding camp until they could be shipped back home to Canada.

In late 1918, under the direction (indeed control) of Paul Konody, a distinguished Canadian art critic and writer, artists (painters) were sought of a high standard to document the war from a totally Canadian perspective. David Milne was being considered for inclusion in this project, but examples of his work for perusal by Konody were all back in the United States. So Milne had about thirty of his paintings shipped over to Britain, a task almost certainly carried out by his long-standing friend James Clarke.

As a result, David B. Milne was selected to be an Official Canadian War Artist, a prestigious honour. Milne began working as a war artist after the Armistice on 11 November 1918 and as he was at Kinmel Camp together with many, many other Canadian soldiers he began his War Artist work at the camp, firstly carrying out preliminary sketches, until on 12 December 1918 he began producing his first work.

Between 12 December 1918 and 1 February 1919 Milne produced twelve works of Kinmel Camp and the area that surrounded it, with not all of the twelve works being individually dated.

R. F. Wodehouse, writing as the Curator of War Art for

Canada in the 1960s, upon looking at Milne's early work at and of Kinmel Camp, proffered : 'There are certain oddities of style in some of these first works which are worth noting. A few of them are reminiscent of the illustrations from the official manual of field sketching. Perhaps he was not sure of what was needed and was feeling his way. On leaving Kinmel Park Camp, his individual style clearly manifests itself'.

So Milne honed his style as an Official Canadian War Artist at Kinmel Camp, before moving on to the painting of works at other military camps in Britain and then on to paint the battlefields of France and Flanders in his own truly unique style. All the military Camps in Britain and all the locations in France and Flanders were where Canadian Troops had trained and and fought.

Today, David B. Milne's paintings of Kinmel Camp, other British military camps, and of France and Flanders form an important and highly respected part of the Canadian War Memorials Collection that is housed in the National Gallery of Canada at the country's capital of Ottawa, and a number of his non war-related paintings are housed in prestigious galleries around the world.

The National Film Board of Canada in Montreal, Quebec, has in its collections a twelve-minute film entitled, 'The World of David Milne' and some of Milne's own letters are used as commentary for the film that sought to show many of his paintings and to provide an insight into his rather unique painting style. Milne's war-related paintings were done in the dry-brush, watercolour technique.

David B. Milne is most certainly not a forgotten artist, with over the years a number of exhibitions of his work being held. When one of his paintings does come up for auction, they sell for very large sums of money. On 29 June 1992, Canada Post issued a fifty-cent postage stamp, 'Red

Nasturtiums', celebrating the David B. Milne painting of 1937, of that title.

On a personal note, of the twelve Kinmel Camp related paintings done by David B. Milne my own two favourites are 'Kinmel Park Camp: The Camp at Night, 12-13 December 1918', and Kinmel Camp: The Concert at the 'Y', 21 December 1918', both watercolour over graphite on wove paper.

An 'Inspector Calls' at Kinmel Park Camp!

J. B. Priestley, world-famous novelist, dramatist, broadcaster and campaigner, was born simply as John Priestley, on 13 September 1894, in Bradford, Yorkshire. John Priestley, known as 'Jack' by family and friends, left Belle Vue Grammar School, Bradford, aged sixteen, and became a junior clerk from 1910 until August of 1914, in the offices of Helm & Co., a wool firm at Swan Arcade, Bradford.

The Swan Arcade was a fine ornate Victorian four-storey office building and shopping arcade located in Bradford City Centre, standing between Market Street and Broadway and opposite the Wool Exchange. Swan Arcade was named after the White Swan Inn that had previously stood on the same site.

John Priestley had a passion for books and bought as many as he could with his then meagre earnings and he began to try his hand at writing. He had a regular (though unpaid) column in the *Bradford Pioneer*, a local Labour Party weekly. Under the heading 'Round the Hearth', he wrote pieces about local concerts and locally performed plays, with his contributions being surrounded by fiercely Socialist articles.

John Priestley's first paid piece of professional writing was an article entitled 'Secrets of The Rag-Time King', which appeared in the *London Opinion* on 14 December

1912. It was to be the start of a long and fine literary career, greatly interrupted by the war.

When war was declared in August 1914, John Priestley was nearly twenty, and he was keen to do his bit, so he enlisted as a Private in his local Duke of Wellington's, 10th Battalion, the West Riding Regiment on 7 August 1914. I believe that it was around this time that he added Boynton as his middle name as his attestation and enlistment forms of 7 August 1914, have him calling himself John Boynton Priestley. He voluntarily enlisted with the innocence and keenness of youth in his then strong belief ('jingoism', as it was called by some), in fighting for king and country and for the British Empire. He was on Home Service undergoing military training until 25 August 1915, some of it at Frensham Camp, near Farnham, Surrey and some at Bramshott Camp, Hampshire.

While on active service in France a dug-out collapsed on him and he was returned home to Britain to convalesce. He was for some weeks a patient at the North Evington War Hospital in Leicester. Priestley then spent some further months in military hospitals before being recommended for, and then receiving a commission in the Devonshire Regiment. He had left Alnwick Camp and was passed fit, 'at last' as he put it, then became temporarily attached to 3rd Battalion on Tyneside, waiting to be sent as a cadet to an Officer Training Corps. In the event, Priestley was sent for his officer training to Kinmel Camp to be in 16th Officer Cadet Battalion.

In his book *Margin Released – reminiscences & reflections*, first published in 1962, Priestley wrote favourably of his time at Kinmel Camp, something he definitely did not do about most of the other military camps and establishments he was at during his time in the army during virtually the entire war. This book is full of his undisguised criticisms of the British Army and particularly of the senior officer class.

Though he always denied the book was an autobiography, it was very close to being such, and is an excellent and honestly written book that encompasses most of his life:

The 16th Officer Cadet Battalion – I think that was its name – to which I was posted, much to my relief, was at Kinmel Park Camp in north Wales. We were worked hard there, but I enjoyed it all. I was jerked out of my apathy, my slack habits of mind and body. I made no close friends among my fellow Cadets – there was hardly time – but they were pleasant to work and live with. The Enemy did not show up among the officers and Instructors. I played football again, for my Company team. I wrote some satirical odds and ends, both for print and for performance. A great deal of what we were taught I could not take seriously, not simply because I was not really a military type, though of course I was not, because I believed much of it to be out of date, merely an attempt to improve on what we had in the Boer War. All that musketry for example, in which one of our chief instructors was a Major in Orders, perhaps a parson-schoolmaster before the war, a cheerful pagan who was fond of referring to 'we old Bisley bullpunchers', hardly an ecclesiastical Order. It seemed to me that the rifle was all very well in frontier skirmishes, but the war we were in was chiefly an affair of machine-guns, bombs, mortars, shellfire. And I had a sharp dislike, together with much mistrust, of all that he-man guff about 'the spirit of the bayonet'. We might have saved about half a million lives if we had forgotten all those campaigns against Fuzzy wuzzies and Boer commanders and had given some thought to the German General Staff. Not that our platoon commander, though an oldish regular, was so limited in his outlook. His name was Tredennick, and he was an odd fish, conscientious but probably a bit cracked, and when he got going on strategy, his eyes glittering and the words pouring out, whole continents, not yet fully involved, rose and took to arms. Asia rushed to meet Africa, and soon we lit our pipes and stayed out of the rain, the globe was on fire. We were back at school, dangling the bait we knew the master could not resist, triumphantly wasting time.

We dined in turn at the Officers' Mess, to prove we did not always eat peas with a knife. We sat for an examination. All but an unfortunate few were passed out and duly commissioned. Out of the allowance we were given we bought greatcoats and British warms, tunics and Sam Browne belts. We were officers free for ever from cookhouse fatigues and carrying coils of barbed wire. I was commissioned to the Devon Regiment, and after a few days' swagger at home I arrived at its headquarters and barracks at Devonport, as new and shy and glossy as a bridegroom.

His comment that 'the Enemy did not show up amongst the Officers and Instructors' at Kinmel Park Camp refers to his great dislike of 'the Enemy', who for him were the pompous, overblown officers and Instructors, many of them bullies, who had themselves seen little or no real action at the Front in the war.

J.B. Priestley left Kinmel Camp as a Second Lieutenant and took up his commission with the Devonshire Regiment, returning to the Front in France with them on 29 January 1918. He managed to survive the War, though like so many who did by its end he had a great distaste, to say the least, for war and militarism. He became a prolific and internationally known novelist, dramatist, critic and broadcaster. Arguably his finest and most famous work is the stage play *An Inspector Calls*, which is performed worldwide even today.

Under-age Abergele soldier Determined to Fight at the Front

Owen Jones was born on 21 August 1900, as Owen Parry, as he was 'born out of wedlock' (as it was called in those days). His Mother, Ann Parry from Llanfairtalhairn, near Abergele, married an Owen Jones from Abergele a few months after Owen's birth, and the boy took the surname of Jones.

Despite his young age, Owen Jones (Junior) was determined to attest and enlist in the army and he wanted to fight the enemy at the Front in France. In around October 1915, aged but fifteen years and two months, he first attested and enlisted in one of the Royal Welch Fusilier Battalions at Kinmel Camp. He became Private Owen Jones, Regimental Number 35546. He gave a false date of birth when attesting and enlisting, but was on this first attempt found out rather easily and discharged from military service due to his age. His Medal Roll Card shows him when with the Royal Welch Fusiliers as a Private, Regimental Number 60180, which perhaps was yet another attempt at attesting and enlisting and getting to the Front.

But not to be deterred, on 17 February 1916, aged fifteen years and six months, he again went along to the nearby Kinmel Camp and attested and enlisted in 13th (Reserve) Battalion, the South Wales Borderers, known as the 4th Gwent. He gave the false age of seventeen years and eleven months and stated that he was a railway labourer. Young Owen Jones became Private Owen Jones, Regimental Number 33353. He was 5' 4" inches tall, but the question is, did he reasonably look to be eighteen years of age to those to whom he attested and enlisted at Kinmel Camp? At this time his parents and siblings were residing at 32 Peel Street, Abergele. This was young Owen Jones' second, possibly third, attempt to get to fight at the Front, but it failed, as his parents got wind of what he was doing. They contacted Abergele solicitor Mr Edward Alfred Crabbe, who was also Clerk to the Abergele Justices, to assist them in stopping their young son from going to fight at the Front, but appear to have had no objection to his being a soldier in the army on Home Service. This letter was sent by Solicitor Mr E. A. Crabbe to – The Officer Commanding, 13th Battalion, the South Wales Borderers, Kinmel Park Camp:

> Town Hall,
> Abergele
> 18 March 1916
>
> Dear Sir,
>
> RE: PRIVATE OWEN JONES. NO. 33353.
> Mr Owen Jones the Father of the above Private has seen me today. It appears that he is not yet 16 years of age & will not be until 21st of August next, that the Lad has gone through his Course & may at any time be put in a draft for the Front. Having regard to his age his parents Naturally Object to his going to the Front. They have no other reasons for Objecting.
>
> With regard to the Lad's age, I believe a Certificate of Birth has been handed in. There may be some confusion by the fact that the Certificate is in the name of 'OWEN PARRY'. The boy was born out of Wedlock & was registered in the Mother's maiden name. The Father did not marry the Mother until 5 months after the birth.
>
> I shall be glad to hear from you upon the matter.
> I am, Sir,

Your obedient servant.

Edward A. Crabbe.

This letter had the desired effect and young Owen Jones was discharged 'Officially' for the first time from military service due to his age, on 16 April 1916.

Owen Jones then made a third (possibly fourth) and fully successful attempt at attesting and enlisting, this time in the Cheshire Regiment. He was now Private Owen Jones, Regimental Number 64619, and this time he got his wish and was sent in a draft of soldiers to the Front in France and Flanders. He eventually found himself at the Front with 11th (Service) Battalion, the Cheshire Regiment, and on 20 April 1918, he was Killed in Action, aged but seventeen years and eight months. He died during what is called the Battles of the Lys, which ostensibly took place between 7 April 1918 and 29 April 1918 and in which 11th Battalion, the Cheshire Regiment sustained heavy losses.

Robert Graves Spent over a Year at Kinmel Park Camp

Robert von Ranke Graves, better known to us as Robert Graves, the poet, novelist, scholar and controversial public figure, spent over one year as an army officer stationed at Kinmel Camp.

Robert Graves was born on 24 July 1895, at the family home of 1, Lauriston Road, Wimbledon, London, to Alfred Perceval Graves, an Inspector of Schools, Editor of a Literary Magazine and published Poet, and his second Wife, Amalie Elizabeth Sophie Graves (nee von Ranke). Alfred Perceval Graves and his first Wife, Jane had five children together before her death in 1886. Alfred then married Amalie, known by friends and family as Amy and they also had five children together, Robert Graves being the third-born of these. The Graves and von Ranke families were packed with a variety of relatives and ancestors who were from a very wide range of upper-middle and upper-class backgrounds, that included intellectuals, lawyers, doctors, clergymen and some military men. Robert Graves was also born of a very mixed European lineage, with English, Scottish, Irish, German and Danish 'blood in his veins'.

The main Graves family home was in Wimbledon, London, but the Graves family were wealthy enough to have built for them, in 1892, a holiday home at Harlech, north Wales, a handsome stone-built, six-bedroomed property which they called Erinfa, set in elevated and substantial grounds. The house commanded wonderful views of the Llŷn peninsula and towards the Snowdon mountain range. Robert Graves had many enjoyable times at Erinfa prior to 1908, particularly when roaming the hills around Harlech with his siblings.

However, in 1908, aged thirteen, Robert Graves was sent to 'purgatory': Charterhouse public school, but for him it truly amounted to a form of living hell. At Charterhouse things were made even more difficult for him when the totally false rumour was circulated that he was of German birth and worse – a German Jew! He was terribly unhappy and was greatly bullied, to such an extent that on at least one occasion when he returned to Erinfa, Harlech, in the school holidays, he was close to a mental breakdown. But he was able to find solace by going on long, solitary walks on the wild and rugged Welsh hills around Harlech. Much of his very early poetry was full of Myth and Magic, engendered largely by these hills. He returned a number of times over the years to Erinfa to 'escape the real world and to re-charge himself', often bringing with him friends who were later to become very famous in their own right.

At Charterhouse, Robert Graves became quite a

proficient boxer and excelled at a number of sports. More importantly for the future, Robert Graves did receive a very sound classical education, however much he loathed the place. Few aspects of public school life pleased him, but he found an unlikely friendship with George Mallory, a young teacher at Charterhouse, who found him interesting enough to take him with him on several climbing trips in Britain, including on occasions to Snowdonia. George Mallory was later to find worldwide fame and indeed acclaim as an accomplished climber, especially in relation to his climbing of Mount Everest.

In July 1913, Robert Graves attended Charterhouse's own Officer Training Corps Summer Camp on Salisbury Plain. At this juncture Robert Graves was no supporter of war, believing it to be a waste of time for educated men.

Somehow Robert Graves did manage to survive the Charterhouse experience with the 'odd hiccup and homosexual incident' on the way, and pleased his parents when getting to St John's College, Oxford in 1914. He did not take up this university place, however, as in the summer of 1914, all hell was let loose with the outbreak of war. Robert Graves was to take an active part in it.

It was through the Secretary of the Royal St David's Golf Club at Harlech that Robert Graves obtained his army commission. After a conversation with Robert Graves and knowing the Graves family quite well, the Secretary of the Golf Club rang the Depot of the Royal Welch Fusiliers at Wrexham, informing them of Robert Graves' Officer Training Corps experience when at Charterhouse and also stating that the Graves family had a strong military background. The latter piece of information was sort of true, but most of these military men were on the von Ranke – German – side of his family! But it worked and on 11 August 1914 Robert Graves presented himself at the Royal Welch

Fusiliers Regimental Headquarters at Wrexham for military service.

Graves' own earlier reticence about a war with Germany and his taking any active part in it virtually evaporated overnight when the German army invaded tiny, neutral Belgium. There was also an element of Robert Graves' enlisting in order to please his family and anyway he thought on 11 August 1914, the War would not last long. He had most certainly not been looking forward to starting at Oxford in the autumn of that year.

Robert Graves and Siegfried Sassoon first met whilst serving together for a brief period as officers in the same Battalion of the Royal Welch Fusiliers. They hit it off straightaway, being from very similar backgrounds, and both writers who had a real passion for poetry. The both of them felt rather alienated in their military surroundings and their 'friendship' (some say that it was more and had for a time a physical sexual element to it) grew, though over the next number of years they fell out on occasions over a range of matters. On at least one occasion Graves took Sassoon back with him to Erinfa, where they pored over their poetry, reading and advising on each other's compositions.

On 6 September 1915, Robert Graves began a ten-day leave which he enjoyed with his family at Erinfa; ten days of normality and home comforts before he had to return to the Front and rejoin his Battalion, who were preparing for a great push against the German lines. This great push was to be the Battle of Loos, which began at 6.30 a.m. on 25 September 1915, along a seven-mile front. It was particularly terrible as regards casualties for the Royal Welch Fusiliers. In the end, the Battle of Loos, whose various actions finally ended on 13 October 1915, had resulted in some 20,000 German casualties, but some 60,000 British casualties, for the gain at best of around 8,000 yards of ground. Robert Graves had managed to come out of it unscathed physically, if not mentally.

Whilst he was in and out of the trenches at the Front in France and Flanders, Robert Graves had published three collections of his poems, namely *Over the Brazier* (1916), *Goliath and David* (1917) and *Fairies and Fusiliers* (1917), the former two being more war-related and the latter having a rather strong sexual element to it, something that was noticed and commented upon by Siegfried Sassoon.

Having survived the Battle of Loos and a number of months at the Front, in July of 1916, during the Somme Offensive, Robert Graves was seriously wounded when shrapnel from an exploding shell pierced his chest and thigh. His wounds were initially medically assessed so serious, together with a dash of administrative confusion, that he was reported as 'Officially Dead, having Died of His Wounds, Received in Action'. Whilst the badly wounded though still very much alive Robert Graves was being transported back to a military hospital in England, his parents were officially informed of his death and his personal belongings he had left behind in France were forwarded to them. An obituary piece for Robert Graves even appeared in *The Times*. Lieutenant-Colonel Crawshay, his Commanding Officer, sent a kindly worded letter of condolence to Robert Graves' mother, informing her on a more personal level of her son's 'death' in the trenches on 22 July 1916:

Dear Mrs Graves,
I very much regret to have to write to you and tell you your son has died of wounds. He was very gallant, and was doing so well and is a great loss.
He was hit by a shell and very badly wounded, and died on the way down to the base I believe. He was

not in bad pain, and our doctor managed to get across and attend to him at once.

We have had a very hard time, and our casualties have been large. Believe me you have all our sympathy in your loss, and we have lost a very gallant soldier.

Please write to me if I can tell you or do anything.

Your sincerely,

C. Crawshay, Lt-Col.

Six or seven officers of the Battalion together with many men had been killed on the same day that Robert Graves was so badly wounded, with only eighty men being left in the Battalion able to report for Duty. Robert Graves underwent hospital treatment and quite a long period of convalescence, with his lungs especially having been very detrimentally affected by the shrapnel from the exploding shell.

Robert Graves was eventually passed at a further medical board as being Category B2, which meant that he was 'fit for garrison service at home'. He was for a short period a Temporary Instructor with No. 4, Officer Cadet Battalion, based at Wadham College, Oxford. Then he moved on to Oswestry Military Camp and then in mid-October 1917, to Kinmel Camp.

A letter dated October 1917, from Robert Graves to fellow army officer and budding poet, Wilfred Owen (Wilfred Edward Salter Owen, born 18 March 1893 at Oswestry, Shropshire) has the senders' address as '3rd Garrison Batt., R.W.F., Kinmel Park, Rhyl, N. Wales'. In this letter Robert Graves commends Wilfred Owen for his latest poem entitled, 'Disabled' and goes on to give some critical, though constructive, advice as to the content of the poem. Robert Graves ends this letter:

Till then, good luck in the good work.
Yours Robert Graves.
Love to Sassoon.

In Robert Graves' book *Goodbye To All That* he refers to
October 1917:

> I reckoned on being sent to the Third Garrison
> Battalion of the Regiment now under canvas at
> Oswestry in Wales. From there, when I felt a bit
> better, I would get myself passed B1, or 'Fit for
> garrison service abroad', and would, in due course, be
> sent to a Royal Welch garrison battalion in Egypt.
> Once there, it should be easy to get passed A1 and
> join the Twenty-fourth or Twenty-fifth (New Army)
> Battalion in Palestine.
>
> So presently I was sent to Oswestry. We had a
> good Colonel, but the men were mostly compulsory
> enlistments, and the officers, with a few exceptions,
> useless. My first task on arrival was to supervise the
> entraining of battalion stores and transport; we were
> moving to Kinmel Park Camp, near Rhyl. The
> adjutant gave me one hundred and fifty men, and
> allowed me six hours for the job. I chose fifty of the
> stronger men, and three or four NCOs who looked
> capable, then sent the remainder away to play
> football. By organizing the mob in First Battalion
> style, I got my fifty men to load the train in two hours
> less than the scheduled time. The Colonel
> congratulated me. At Rhyl, he gave me the job of
> giving 'further instruction' to the sixty or so young
> officers sent to him from the cadet-battalions. Few
> officers in the battalion had seen any active service.

After a short period of leave for his marriage in January 1918 to
Nancy Nicholson, he being twenty-two and she only eighteen
years of age, life reverted back to before they were married:

> A week later, Nancy returned to her farm, and I to my
> command at Kinmel Park. It was an idle life now. No
> men attended parade; all were employed on camp
> duties. And I found a Lieutenant with enough
> experience to attend to the 'further instruction' of the
> young officers. My orderly room took about ten
> minutes each day; crime was rare, and the adjutant
> always kept ready and in order the few documents to
> be signed; which left me free to ride all my three
> chargers over the countryside, in turn, for the rest of
> the day.

Further extracts taken from *Goodbye To All That*:

> Wearying of this idleness, I arranged to be transferred
> to the Sixteenth Officer Cadet Battalion in another
> part of the same camp. There I did the same sort of
> work as with the Fourth at Oxford, and stayed from
> February 1918 until the Armistice in November 11th.
> Rhyl being much healthier than Oxford, I could play
> games without danger of another break-down. Nancy
> got a job at a market-gardener's near the camp, and
> came up to live with me. A month or two later she
> found that she was having a baby, stopped land work,
> and went back to her drawing.
>   Armistice-night hysteria did not touch our camp
> much, though some of the Canadians stationed there
> went down to Rhyl to celebrate in true overseas style.
> The news sent me out walking alone along the dyke
> above the marshes of Rhuddlan (an ancient

battlefield, the Flodden of Wales), cursing, and sobbing and thinking of the dead.

Siegfried's famous poem celebrating the Armistice began:

> Everybody's suddenly burst out singing,
> And I was filled with such delight
> As prisoned birds must find in freedom… …

But 'everybody' did not include me.

With the Armistice on 11 November 1918, and the war over, Kinmel Camp was about to change from a wartime training camp to a transit camp. Thousands of Canadian soldiers were to be billeted there to await repatriation:

> In the middle of December the cadet battalion's were wound up, and the officers, after a few days leave, sent back to their units. I had orders to rejoin the Royal Welch Third Battalion, now at Castle Barracks, Limerick, but decided to overstay my leave until the baby was born. Nancy expected it early in January 1919.

In October of 1919, Robert Graves took up his place at Oxford, changing his course after a short period to English Language and Literature. Due to his poor health he was permitted to live outside Oxford itself, choosing Boars Hill, a hilly hamlet three miles south-west of Oxford. Here the residents included his Landlord, the Poet and Writer, John Masefield, who later from 1930, until his death in 1967, was the Poet Laureate of the United Kingdom. Graves and his family later moved to reside at Worlds End Cottage, which was on Collice Street, Islip, in Oxfordshire. Whilst studying at Oxford, Graves' most notable companion and friend was T. E. Lawrence, better known, perhaps, as 'Lawrence of Arabia'. They met when Lawrence was at Oxford as a Research Fellow and at the same time serving as a political advisor to the Middle East Department of the British Colonial Office. Graves' first commercial success was a biography of Lawrence, published in 1927, entitled, *Lawrence and the Arabs*. In 1929, Graves' fine, well-regarded, though controversial, autobiography was published – *Goodbye To All That*, a book that gave him real financial security. Robert Graves is also today remembered for his Great War poetry, and for his *I Claudius* and *Claudius the God*, which in the 1970s were turned into a highly successful BBC television drama series.

Robert Graves' poem 'The Welsh Incident', originally published in 1929, then entitled 'The Railway Carriage', has in its lines mentions of Cricieth, Caernarvon, Pwllheli, Tremadoc, Penrhyndeudraeth and Borth. The great Welsh actor, Richard Burton was recorded reciting this poem, in his inimitable way. I have had the pleasure of listening to this recording and also one of Robert Graves himself reciting the poem in a Welsh-sounding accent.

Robert Graves died of heart failure on 7 December 1985 at Deja, Majorca, aged ninety. He was buried the next morning in the small churchyard set on a hill at Deja.

6

Conscientious Objectors at Kinmel Park Camp

The first that was publicly heard of Conscientious Objectors being at Kinmel Camp was when on 12 April 1916, various newspapers ran the story of two unnamed Non-Combatant soldiers at the camp, being court-martialled there and as a result each man being sentenced to two-years imprisonment with hard labour. Kinmel Camp was one of Britain's primary military establishments to which men who were Conscientious Objectors were sent after they had lost their appeals at local tribunals for exemption from military service. The aim being to coerce them at the military establishment into compliance, namely to become soldiers.

By late 1915 Britain was suffering very heavy war casualties. The volunteers to replace them were drying up and were proving not to be enough. The compulsory call-up of British men was an inevitability, and as a result, the pacifist members of the No-Conscription Fellowship (NCF), which had with foresight been set up earlier in 1915, successfully campaigned to secure a clause in the 1916 Military Service Act (which brought in Military Conscription) the right to claim exemption from military service under certain conditions.

The man in question, having been called up, would be required to attend a local tribunal at which his claim for exemption was to be 'fairly assessed on humane grounds'. That was the theory as far as the Government was 'officially' concerned, but local tribunals were made up of individual human beings with their own thoughts and opinions, a really mixed bunch of people, shopkeepers and businessmen, civil servants, landowners, retired military officers, most of them too old to be called up themselves for military service. Plus on each local tribunal sat one member selected by the army, known as the Military Representative. This Military Representative had the right at every hearing to cross-examine each and every applicant, which they invariably did with vigour and with of course one quite obvious aim – to get as many of the applicants for exemption from military service into the military as they could! I was surprised to learn, considering that period and women not having the vote yet, that some local tribunals included women; it was said they were often the most scathing of local tribunal members towards applicants for exemption. Probably many of these women had husbands, sons or other close relatives already serving in the military.

The Conscientious Objectors, COs for short, came from many walks of life and from the different echelons of society. At some local tribunals which were covered by the press, the applicant would be verbally harangued and in some cases not even allowed to speak at the hearing, whilst other perhaps more erudite applicants put forward eloquent and reasoned statements in support of their claims for exemption. Only a small minority received full exemption with most being denied any exemption whatsoever. In total some 16,000 British men were to make a claim for permanent exemption and this was the regular cycle of events once the local tribunal had refused them any form of exemption:

The refused applicant would then appeal, which almost always failed. Then a civilian police officer would call at the man's home and formally arrest him on a charge of 'Being a Deserter from the Army', as he had failed to respond to his call-up papers or present himself physically for military service as required. He would then appear before a Local

Magistrates Court, which would usually consist of people even more difficult to appeal to than the local tribunal! The Conscientious Objector (CO) was then usually fined around forty shillings (£2), which was to be deducted from his future army pay! The Court would then hand the CO officially over to a military escort which then promptly would take the CO to the chosen military establishment, which, for many from as far afield as Newport, south Wales and Blackburn in Lancashire, would be Kinmel Camp, north Wales.

These Conscientious Objectors were required to carry out such 'expected soldierly duties' as to wear the army uniform of the Regiment or Corps they had been assigned to, to go on parade or take part in weapons training etc. When they refused to obey these instructions, usually given initially by an NCO (a Non-Commissioned Officer), a Commissioned Officer would then Order the CO to carry out these instructions, with failure to do so resulting in the CO being charged with disobedience and placed in detention in a Guard Room, to await the convening of a court martial. The court martial would then take place quite promptly at the military Establishment in question and always disregarded any and every claim of the CO to being a civilian, a pacifist or whatever! He was found guilty and sentenced to various terms of imprisonment with hard labour. Usually a few months on the first occasion, but after the initial court martial usually to 112 days or to two years, to be served at a civilian prison, not a military one, even though the 'alleged offences' were all military ones. Now comes the vicious cycle! When the Conscientious Objector (CO), better known colloquially by the English and Welsh public and press as Conchie or Conshi, had served his prison sentence he was returned to the army and taken back to Kinmel Camp or a similar military establishment and then the whole process would begin again. A Superior Officer would Order him to put on his army uniform and he would refuse etc. etc. etc.

Not all the Conscientious Objectors fell into the same category. There were three main types: namely the Absolutists, the Alternativists and the Non-Combatants:

Absolutists – (Often called 'out-and-outers') These were opposed totally to conscription and to the war; most of these were pacifists, but others had other objections, such as unwillingness to fight against fellow-Socialists.

Alternativists – These were prepared to undertake civilian type work, not under any kind of military control, and local tribunals did have the authority to exempt men from military service on condition that they carried out such work.

Non-Combatants – These men were prepared to accept being called-up, but refused in any way to be trained to use weapons or anything to do with weapons. Again, the local tribunals had the authority to put these men on the military register as Non-Combatants, which did often happen. The British press coined the term for these men not as being in the Non- Combatant Corps, but in the 'No Courage Corps'; this often for stretcher-bearers and ambulance drivers at the Front was a most undeserved jibe, for the work they carried out, risking their lives every bit as much on occasions as the combatant soldiers – even in the highly dangerous task of bomb disposal.

The local newspapers reported that in late May of 1916, a considerable number of Conscientious Objectors were taken away from Kinmel Camp to civilian prisons. One newspaper estimated the number to have been between seventy and eighty. These men having been tried by court martial and sentenced to up to two years imprisonment for refusing to obey orders. It was said that these COs had whilst at the camp absolutely refused to obey orders. Some of them having even declined to shave, attend parade or put on the khaki uniform clothing that they had been issued with. One of these men had apparently just sat around Kinmel Camp for long periods in his pyjamas after his civilian clothing had been taken away from him and he had been placed under arrest and removed to the guardroom whilst in that condition.

The newspapers were eager to show that there was no love lost between the soldiers in uniform at Kinmel Camp and the Conscientious Objectors there. It was reported that a group of Conscientious Objectors were en route on a Monday from Kinmel Camp to civilian prisons, when one of the Silver Bands at the camp struck up 'the Dead March in Saul' as they passed-by, as a sign of their feelings in the matter!

However, a number of local newspapers and some further afield, such as the *Evening Telegraph*, Scotland, and the *Essex Newsman*, reported that a further seven Conscientious Objectors at Kinmel Camp had been court-martialled, but these men were actually named. This is what the *Western Daily Press* reported on Friday 2 June 1916:

> A court martial at Kinmel Park, Abergele, north Wales, has sentenced Dorian Herbert, J. H. Davies, G. W. Reynolds, P. Pope, T. C. Griffiths, A. Rudall and A. J. Hewinson, Conscientious Objectors from Newport, to two years' hard labour for refusing to obey the orders of a superior officer.

The *Merthyr Pioneer* of 10 June 1916 covered the same basic story, but with one major addition, a letter from one of these seven Conscientious Objectors:

NEWPORT N.C.F'ERS.
NINE SOUTH WALIANS SENT TO
WORMWOOD SCRUBS.

Comrades Percy Pope, Albert Rudall, Arthur J. Hewinson, G.Reynolds, Dorian Herbert, J. H. Davies, Trevor C. Griffiths (all of the Newport Independent Labour Party and No-Conscription Fellowship Branches). Joseph Shepherd (Pontypridd), and W.T. Jones (Treforest) were on Friday removed from Kinmel Park to Wormwood Scrubs to commence their period of two years' hard labour for 'disobeying in such a manner as to show wilful defiance of authority a lawful command given personally by his superior officer in the execution of his office'.

The following is a copy of the 'official letter' which has been received from Arthur Hewinson. The whole form is printed, and all that has to be filled in by the correspondent is the state of health, and the period which must elapse before a letter can be written. In this case the words, 'My sentence is two years', were added in writing:

H.M. Prison, Wormwood Scrubs, June 3, 1916,
Dear Father, – I am now in this prison, and I am in usual health. If I behave well I shall be allowed to write a letter about 7 weeks' time and to receive a reply, but no reply is allowed to this. My sentence is two years.
Signature, ARTHUR HEWINSON.
Register No. 350.

It is no surprise to learn of an enclave of Conscientious Objectors in the Newport, south Wales area, as one of the two Founders of the No-Conscription Fellowship (NCF) was Reginald Clifford Allen, who was born and bred in Newport. Indeed many of the roots of the opposition to the war in Britain emanated from Wales – south Wales and people with profound Labour and/or Socialist values and views.

Of these seven Newport men, 'named and shamed' by the various newspapers the length and breadth of Britain but treated far more equitably by the staunch Labour Party and Trade Union movement-supporting *Merthyr Pioneer*, one of them was to die before the war ended as a direct result of his treatment by the authorities, both military and civilian, for his Conscientious Objection.

This man was the A. Rudall/Albert Rudall of the two newspaper articles above. He was Albert Rudall, born in 1887 at Newport. Albert Rudall had absolutely no intention of volunteering or otherwise for military service during the war. However, when conscription was first introduced he was required now by law, due to his age and marital status, to enlist in the military. At this time he was residing at 148, Shaftesbury Street, Newport. He resolutely refused to enlist, and on his Army B 2513 Enlistment Form, the word 'Enlistment' is well crossed out. Albert Rudall refused to declare if he was married or not and refused to sign the form as was required of him.

He then appeared before a local tribunal to appeal, but they refused his appeal and stated that he had to now enlist. He was formally arrested a few weeks later by a local police officer and taken before the local Magistrate's Court. There he informed the court that he refused to enlist, citing his conscientious objection, and was fined the usual forty shillings (£2) for being an absentee. On 2 May 1916, he was sent to Kinmel Camp as Private Albert Rudall, Regimental Number 46100, in 20th Battalion, the Royal Welch Fusiliers. The military authorities were determined to make him into a soldier; he was determined to resist them in every way possible, declaring all along that he was a Conscientious Objector.

Albert Rudall's Army Service Record (parts of it, in the incorrect name of Albert Ruddale) has officially stamped across the front sheet in black ink capital letters 'DISCHARGED' and is a litany of refusing to co-operate with the military authorities at Kinmel Camp, especially disobeying the orders of a Superior Officer. Then on 25 May 1916, at Kinmel Camp, he went before a court martial and was handed a sentence of two years' imprisonment with hard labour. At the same time he was transferred to 63rd Training Reserve Battalion, as Private Number TR/4/24729. On 28 May 1916, his court martial sentence was remitted to 112 days' imprisonment with hard labour. Albert Rudall was then transferred in and out of other Training Reserve Battalions until he ended up in a civilian prison, doing hard labour, and by all accounts it was ensured that his time in prison, as it was for most of the imprisoned Conscientious Objectors, would be a very difficult one, where he would be regarded as much worse by the civilian prison authorities and their prison staff than the lowest common criminal, and be treated as such.

Albert Rudall died in October of 1918, aged thirty, due, according to a number of reliable sources, to the terrible treatment meted out to him during his brief army service, then imprisonment in civilian prisons with harsh treatment and poor food, followed by being forced to carry out hard manual labour or face being returned to a civilian prison. The *Merthyr Pioneer* of 19 October 1918 published this piece in tribute to him on its front page following his death:

IN MEMORIAM
DEATH OF ALBERT RUDALL, C.O.
We regret to announce the death of Albert Rudall of

Newport, Mon. Comrade Rudall was an old ILP'er and one of the original COs arrested under the Military Service Act. After his imprisonment he was released on to the Home Office Scheme and worked at Keddington, Warwick and Dartmoor. A short while ago he was allowed to proceed home to find work under the H.O. New Scheme of Exceptional Employment and owing to the time limit imposed in such cases, was compelled to take work for which he was entirely unsuited. The result is he has left us for good. His Comrades are full of grief at the loss of so sincere, unassuming, but enthusiastic a supporter of freedom and International Brotherhood – a grief which we feel sure will be reflected throughout the whole C.O. movement.

Albert Rudall was one of a total of seventy-three Conscientious Objectors whose deaths can be directly attributed to their mistreatment, both physical and mental during the First World War.

A new tack was then taken by the authorities in regard to the more determind of Conscientious Objectors, by sending a batch of them to the Front in France and have them refuse to obey orders in a War Zone! This article appeared on 26 August 1916 in the *Evening Post*, Wellington, New Zealand and makes mention of Kinmel Camp. It was perhaps more candid in its content as it was not a British Newspaper:

SENTENCED TO DEATH
CONSCIENTIOUS OBJECTORS
HOW DEALT WITH IN FRANCE
Mr Tennant, in the House of Commons, replying to a number of questions, said it was a fact that courts martial held in France had in the exercise of their

judicial functions, sentenced to death certain men, described as Conscientious Objectors, for offences so punishable under the Army Act.

In all these cases, 34 in number, the sentences had been commuted to penal servitude, and the statutory provision, that such sentences must be undergone in the United Kingdom, would be given effect to.

Replying to Mr Chancellor, Mr Tennant said wilful disobedience of orders, though not in the face of the enemy, was punishable by death.

Colonel Norton Griffiths asked why these men were not shot, like other soldiers, for disobeying orders?

Mr King asked if they were to understand that these men, of a non-combatant corps, were in a combatant corps?

Mr Tennant replied in the negative.

In connection with Mr Tennant's statement reported above, the Friend's Service Committee sent out some details. It is possible, the committee stated, to give particulars of the thirty Conscientious Objectors in France, who, it is known, were awaiting sentence, besides the four following: H. C. Marten (Quaker), H. W. Scullard (Congregationalist), J. R. King (Socialist) and J. Foister (Socialist). The additional names are: C. Barritt (Quaker), H. E. Stanton (Quaker), H. E. Hicks, Adam Priestly (in association with Friends, and at one time member of the Friends' Ambulance Unit, of Stafford), Oscar G. Ricketts, B. Bonner (International Bible Student), and H. F. Brewster.

All these men were sent from Harwich and Felixstowe (where most had been sentenced to 28 days detention, and had been on bread and water, and in irons).

The following were sent to France from Richmond (Yorkshire) on 29 May: W.E. Law, A. G. Law, L. Renton, C. A. Senior, C. R. Jackson, S. Hall, C. Hall (International Bible Student, C. Cartwright, E. S. Spencer, J. W. Routledge, C. E. Cryer, A. Myers, R. A. Lown, J. H. Brocklesby, A. Marlew, and N. Gaudie (Congregationalist Adult School scholar and well-known footballer).

The following seven were sent from Salford on 30 May: A. W. Taylor, W. T. Frear, G. H. S. Beavis, E. H. Walker, A. F. Walling, J. F. Murfin, and P. B. Jordan (I.B.S.A.).

Three men have already been sentenced to a year's imprisonment with hard labour, and two, to two years. On Friday last they were still in a military prison in France, although sentenced at the beginning of June. The three men given one year are: Rendel H. Wyatt (master in a Quaker school), J. B. Lief, H. J. Willson.

The 'two year' men are Helsby and Rowlands. These two men were sent out with a draft of the Non-Combatants Corps from Kinmel Park.

Practically all these men are members of the No-Conscription Fellowship.

So just who were the two 'two year' men Helsby and Rowlands sent out with a draft of the Non-Combatant Corps from Kinmel Park to France and had initially been under a sentence of death?

They were in fact Arthur Helsby from St Helens and Charles Rowlands from Bootle, though the latter named was born and bred in Llannor, near Pwllheli, north Wales.

Arthur Helsby was born on 5 September 1889, at 26, Quarry Road, West Derby, Liverpool, to George Helsby, a

Coachman (Domestic) and his Wife, Margaret. In 1901, the family resided at 49, Kinmel Street, Toxteth Park, Liverpool. By 1911, Arthur Helsby, now aged twenty one, a Lithographer by profession and his family were residing at 2, Cairo Street, Thatto Heath, St Helens, Lancashire.

Arthur Helsby was not what you might call 'the usual kind of Conscientious Objector' when he was called-up for military service, his objection was political more than anything else. Arthur Helsby due to his strongly held Communist and Socialist beliefs did not believe in fighting his fellow working class man and believed the War was nothing to do with the ordinary Men and Women of Europe, but a War between the Royalty and Upper Classes of Britain and Germany. Arthur Helsby went through the 'usual Conscientious Objector rigmarole', being required to attest and enlist in the Military. The failed appeal to the local tribunal, with the word 'Enrolment' being crossed off on his official Enrolment Paper. This Army document being officially stamped where it stated Corps joined, 'NON-COMBATANT CORPS'. Though written in the space on the form asking his preference as to which branch of the military he preferred to join was written R.A.M.C. (Royal Army Medical Corps). Arthur Helsby's Army Service Record shows that he arrived at Kinmel Camp on 25 March 1916.

Arthur Helsby had already became of interest to the Authorities in Britain when he made visits to the Communist Club at 18, Park Street, Hazel Grove, Stockport, which had first opened in February 1914. The Police made two separate raids on this Communist Club in Hazel Grove, one in late 1915 and one early in 1916. On one of these raids they arrested a total of four men, one of whom was Arthur Helsby. The Chief Constable had this to say about this arrest of one Arthur Helsby: 'Helsby failed to give an account of himself and was evidently a man of foreign extraction and was removed for further enquiries'. The Authorities regarded him as a subversive, but he most certainly was not a man of foreign extraction, but British born and bred!

The other 'two year man' was Charles Rowlands, who was born in 1887 at Llannor, near Pwllheli, north Wales, to Robert Rowlands, an Agricultural Labourer and his Wife, Laura. In 1891 and still in 1901, the Rowlands family resided at Gate Wen, Llannor.

Charles Rowlands moved to live and work in Lancashire and at the time he was called-up for military service he was a Cotton Salesman, residing at 5, Park Grove, Bootle, Lancashire. He declined to attest and enlist and his Enrolment Papers bear all the hallmarks of an enforced enlistment. In the section for what branch of the Armed Services he preferred to join is written 'No Branch Chosen'. After the usual failed appeal at a Local tribunal, Charles Rowlands was posted to Western Command and on 6 May 1916, he joined the Non-Combatant Corps at Kinmel Camp, as Private, Service Number 911. On 30 May 1916, he was sent out to join the British Expeditionary Force (B.E.F.) in France and only a few days later was initially under a Sentence of Death, commuted to two years imprisonment with hard labour, to be served in a Civilian prison back in Britain.

The *Merthyr Pioneer* of 14 October 1916 had a story concerning two more COs and Kinmel Camp:

Abertillery News
Mr E. H. Wilson, an Abertillery, C.O. who was sentenced to twelve months imprisonment at Kinmel Park on September 25, was removed to Wormwood

Scrubs on Friday, the 29 inst., to undergo his sentence. On the same train for the same destination was Mr W. G. Arrowsmith (from Merthyr), who, after doing four months imprisonment at Cardiff Gaol, was handed to Cardiff Barracks on September 18 and then taken to Kinmel Park where he was court-martialled for the second time and sentenced to two years imprisonment.

Ernest Henry Wilson was a twenty-nine year old ironmonger in Abertillery, south Wales. He was a leading member of the Independent Labour Party (ILP), being its Secretary, and he was also a keen worker in the Abertillery branch of the No-Conscription Fellowship (NCF). Several of his letters were published in the *Merthyr Pioneer,* including one in their 30th September 1916 edition that extolled his belief that his being an Absolutist CO was the only proper way to do things. Not everyone agreed with his stance, however.

The *Merthyr Pioneer* continued to publish, much no doubt to the chagrin of the authorities, military and civil, on a very regular basis, information and updates on Conscientious Objectors from south Wales and their letters, many of them written from guardrooms at Kinmel Camp. This piece on 14 October 1916 revealed that there was some degree of rancour between at least one prominent 'out and outer' Conscientious Objector (E. H. Wilson) and those who bent a little and were prepared to be in one of the Non-Combatant Corps (NCC) or in this case a CO who appreciated that not all were or could be 'Out and Outers' – Absolutists.

THE NCC AND THE CO
To the Editor of the *Pioneer.*
Sir, Will you be good enough to allow a short comment on Comrade Wilson's letter contained in

your issue of the 30 ult. However justifiable his strictures concerning the difference between those who have accepted the N.C.C. position and the 'out and outers' (of whom I am one) may be, I respectfully submit that Comrade Wilson was ill-advised to publish them in his letter. Only one who is in a position to know the intimate affairs of each man who has accepted N.C.C. work can claim to judge them, and even he would hestitate.

As one who has shared their hut – and who is now dependent upon them still for practically everything – I must aver that they have quite satisfactory reasons for having adopted their present attitude, and that, while they have felt unable to go the whole way with others of us, they have given us every possible encouragement and help in our fight.

Thanks largely to them, the life of the 'out and outer' at Kinmel Park is a comparative heaven on earth.

South Walians will be interested to know that in our company are Charles Black, B.A., of Liverpool, and Herbert B. Clarke, of Manchester, I am being court-martialled on Tuesday next.

Last Wednesday the three of us received solitary confinement on bread and water, for refusing to accept the title of Private when addressed by the colonel, he being under the impression that we were showing disrespect. Explanations followed yesterday, and the colonel accepted our assurance that no disrespect was intended, and quite a friendly atmosphere prevailed. Best wishes for the 'Pioneer' – Yours etc.

ARCHIE B. MOON

(Newport, Mon. I.L.P.)

Hut 24, Camp 19, Kinmel Park, Oct. 4, 1916

The *Merthyr Pioneer* of Saturday 4 November 1916 had this rather confident and cheeky piece within it:

CORRESPONDENCE
MARCHING TUNE OF KINMEL CAMP
To the Editor of the *Pioneer*,
Sir, There are ten of us who are now awaiting removal to Wormwood Scrubs and I have just set the following words to a well known tune as our 'detention song':

> We'll sing in jubilation,
> We'll march behind the band,
> With Clifford Allen leading,
> We'll make a glorious stand,
> And when we come from Wormwood,
> Lloyd George will have to say –
> By jove, they're hot,
> This C.O. lot,
> And they have won the day.

Yours, & C., I. Gwynne Rees
Detention Hut 24, Camp 19,
Kinmel Park, October 30 1916.

The *Merthyr Pioneer* of 24 February 1917 had this account of another prominent CO:

Mr Nicholas Again Arrested
Mr Nun Nicholas has been arrested for the second time. Mr Nicholas had been granted (it is stated) four days' leave by the authorities at Wakefield Work Centre, but he extended the leave to one of about six weeks' duration. Some time ago he received a communication from the Home Office commanding

him to return to Wakefield the following day, otherwise he would be arrested. Nun ignored the warning, and ten days later he was arrested and taken to Cardiff Prison, where he now is. Whilst at home he was not inactive in the Labour Movement. He delivered two brilliant lectures before the Swansea Industrial History Class on 'The Tribal System in Wales'. He also spoke at the inaugural meeting of the Clydach Trades Council. Also he delivered the opening lecture for the Clydach Industrial History Class. At Glais he gave a most humorous account of his experiences at Kinmel Park and Wormwood Scrubs.

Nun Nicholas, it would appear was able to bear his terms of imprisonment and the harsh treatment that came with it for his conscientious objection with fortitude, even being able to find some humour in it.

Another prominent south Wales CO was Mansel Grenfell. Mansel Grenfell became a particularly well known CO (publicly as well as in the CO Movement) greatly aided by the coverage of his 'struggle with the Authorities' that appeared from time to time in the *Merthyr Pioneer*. This is from their edition of 14 July 1917:

COURT-MARTIAL OF MANSEL GRENFELL
Second Sentence Of Two Years' Hard Labour
His Statement Before The Court

Since the above reached us Mansel Grenfell has been 'rushed through Kinmel Park', as he himself describes it, and has been re-sentenced to two years hard labour for refusing to obey the 'orders of his superior officer'. Mansel only arrived at the camp at 5 a.m. on Sunday,

June 24, was court-martialled on Thursday, 'read out' on Friday, and was removed to Rhyl, en-route to Walton Gaol, before 7 0'clock on Saturday morning. In sending us a copy of his statement to the court martial, Mansel says:

> I may say it was listened to attentively and courteously. My sentence all the same is two years, Hard Labour! – which I face with perfect calm and confidence. From what I have been able to gather from the few papers I have seen, I think prospects are fine. It is only necessary that we should go on carrying on loyally inside and outside prisons and guardrooms, etc! Yours with fraternal greetings,
> MANSEL GRENFELL

7

Trouble Erupts at Kinmel Park Camp:
Armistice Day 1918 Onwards

At the beginning of November 1918, Kinmel Camp in the main consisted of Officer Cadet Battalions 16 and 17, made up of experienced NCOs and Warrant Officers with War experience, all of whom had been recommended for Commissions to become officers – 'temporary gentlemen', as these men from the ranks were often called. Together with the officers (one was Robert Graves) and Instructors of these two OCB's.

Also at Kinmel Camp was a Queen Mary's Army Auxiliary Depot, with a number of WAACs. Plus a Canadian Young Soldiers' Battalion, about one-third of whom had despite being under-age to do so, already done Active Service at the Front, and some had even been awarded medals for bravery.

On 11 November 1918, came the armistice. The war had been 'won', of course, by Britain and its Allies, but at a catastrophic cost in human and animal life and suffering on both sides, plus enormous financial cost.

To celebrate the armistice, a large contingent of Canadian soldiers at Kinmel Camp, many of them young, but who had fought at the Front, decided to make their way to nearby Rhyl. In late afternoon they piled onto a Kinmel Camp Railway train bound for the seaside resort. On their return to Kinmel Camp on the last train of the evening, many were not surprisingly the worse for drink and had full bottles of liquor with them to continue the revelries inside the camp itself. Canadian soldier, Lance-Corporal John Babcock recalled the events of armistice evening in Kinmel Camp:

We were there when the Armistice was signed on November 11 1918. We got into a beef with some British soldiers and they armed themselves with rifles and bayonets. One fellow got a little obstreperous and they stuck a bayonet through his thigh.

Lance-Corporal John Babcock described the Canadian soldiers with whom he served at that time as, 'a Wild Bunch'.

A happier account appeared days later in the local newspapers from Rhyl residents who stated that on armistice night, hundreds of Canadian soldiers from Kinmel Camp were in Rhyl to celebrate and that they had formed long crocodiles (like our conga dance today) which weaved through the streets of Rhyl.

Continuing Skirmishes at Kinmel Park Camp

Almost every day, beginning on Armistice Day, 11 November 1918, there was trouble inside Kinmel Camp, mainly between the thousands of Canadian soldiers there (15,000 to 20,000 at any one time) and British soldiers, many of whom were there to maintain order and discipline within the camp.

Canadian soldiers were stuck in the camp for days, weeks and into months, longing for repatriation to their own country, keen to return home to see their loved ones and pick up their lives again. So who could blame them in the circumstances for being angry and awkward? Over the centuries most victorious armies have had serious discipline problems once victory had been achieved – it was no exception at Kinmel Camp. The winter of 1918–1919 was a particularly harsh one as locals would later attest. The individual wooden huts at Kinmel Camp that formerly housed thirty men to each one (this was crowded) now were expected to house around forty-two men. This required the taking of turns in sleeping on the floor of the wooden huts. The bitterly cold winter winds were blowing off the nearby sea along the virtually flat plain to the camp. The standard of food provided post-armistice was said to have seriously deteriorated from the pre-armistice days. In late 1918, it was described by some of the Canadian soldiers housed there as being no better than pigswill. The Canadian soldiers were often short of money, many fearing quite correctly that what few jobs were available in Canada would be taken by those who got home promptly – first come, first served!

This early discontent was 'inadvertently' exacerbated when in the following week after the Armistice, the Canadian Young Soldiers at the camp were given an advance in their army pay which they promptly went out and spent on alcohol in nearby Rhyl or in the 'wet canteens' of the camp itself. In these conditions serious trouble flared up in Kinmel Camp on the evening of 20 November 1918, when Canadian soldiers returned to camp and were reunited with ones already in camp. A serious confrontation broke out and one soldier wrote that he feared the wooden huts would so easily go on fire if matters got truly out of hand. It all began when a group of Canadian soldiers having apparently been invited to a 'do' in one of the large entertainment huts by women at the camp (probably WAACs), but were turned away brusquely by some British soldiers at the event. The Canadians regarded it as a snub and proceeded to smash some windows at the hut. An account of this particularly evening was also later given by a Staff Sergeant J. H. Sharpley. Eventually quelled, all the Canadian units involved in the 'trouble' were quickly moved out elsewhere.

The Camp Commandant was the highly regarded war hero and experienced Canadian soldier, Colonel Malcolm

A. Colquhoun, C.M.G., D.S.O., who had been at Kinmel Camp since September 1918. He was only too aware that from Armistice Day, Kinmel Camp was now but a transit camp, a temporary holding camp, for the repatriation of thousands of Canadian soldiers for whom the return to their homeland was now all they craved – and as soon as possible!

These discipline problems and relatively small-scale disturbances were a pre-cursor to the shocking events that were to occur in the camp on 4 March, going into the following day. Described by the military authorities as nothing less than a mutiny by large numbers of Canadian soldiers in the camp, the result was that five of the alleged "mutineers or rioters" were killed, with many on both sides being injured and much damage caused to property in the camp. Shots were fired and there was great violence on both sides. Fifty-one of the alleged "mutineers/rioters" were subsequently tried for a variety of offences and many received long custodial sentences. The court proceedings bore little resemblance to natural justice. The repercussions of these highly controversial events are still debated today and the Kinmel Park camp riots of 1919 have been the subject of a book and a television drama, with a great deal of rancour and debate on the matter existing in the intervening years. Four of the Canadian soldiers who were killed are buried in the nearby St. Margaret's, Bodelwyddan, whilst the body of the fifth was returned to Canada for burial.

Further Reading

Robert Graves, *Goodbye To All That* (London, revised edition 1957)

Julian Putkowski, *The Kinmel Park Camp Riots*, 1919 (Flintshire Historical Society, 1989)

Private Frank Richards, *Old Soldiers Never Die* (Uckfield, n.d.)

Lieut.-Colonel J. E. Munby, *A History of the 38th Welsh Division* (Uckfield, n.d.)

Max Arthur, *Symbol of Courage: the Men Behind the Medal* (London, updated version, 2005)

David P. Silcox, *Painting Place: the Life and Work of David B. Milne* (Toronto, 1996)

J. B. Priestley, *Margin Released* (London, 1962)

Edmund Blunden, *Undertones of War* (London, 2000)

Winston Graham, *Memoirs of a Private Man* (London, 2003)

Helen McPhail and Philip Guest, *On the Trail of the Poets of the Great War: Graves and Sassoon* (Barnsley, 2001)

Acknowledgements

My sister-in-law, Sarah Jones, Denbigh, for her sketch plan of Kinmel Park Camp, 1915 to 1918, that appears so prominently in this book.

Philip G. Hindley – article 'The Kinmel Camp Railway', Issue 102, September 1985 of *The Industrial Railway Record* magazine – courtesy of the Industrial Railway Society (the IRS).

The Kinmel Camp Railway sketch plan: this Roger West drawing copyright The Industrial Railway Society.

The staff at The Denbighshire Records Office/Archives, Ruthin Gaol, 46, Clwyd Street, Ruthin.

The staff at The Flintshire Records Office, The Old Rectory, Rectory Lane, Hawarden.

The YMCA (Mr. Ken Montgomery, Head of International Affairs – YMCA, England), for copyright permission for the reproducing of six YMCA photographs/postcards of Kinmel Park Camp.

The photograph of the party of Royal Engineers working on the Kinmel Camp railway is reproduced, courtesy of Conwy Archive Service.

The photographs of the gravestones of John Victor Hawkins and Lt Arthur Lloyd are reproduced, courtesy of The War Graves Photographic Project.

The Commonwealth War Graves Commission.

Hansard – Historic Hansard Records.

The London Gazette.

The National Archives, Kew, Richmond, Surrey.

The Imperial War Museum.

On-line Shop

Our whole catalogue of titles are
available on our website

- Walking and Mountaineering
- Regions of Wales/Local Guides
- Maritime Wales
- Welsh Heritage and Culture
- Art and Photography
- Welsh History and Myths
- Children's Books

* BARGAINS *

www.carreg-gwalch.com

Walks, History and Heritage

Visit our website for further information:
www.carreg-gwalch.com

Orders can be placed on our
On-line Shop

Further enjoyable reading on History and Heritage